"More of us than ever before are entering what will be the longest stage of our lives—life after sixty. We had maps and role models to guide us through our young adult years and midlife, but where are the maps for our sixties, seventies, and eighties? For women in these age groups, *Wise Choices* describes the territory in high detail.

"How can we get older with passion and purpose, and stay connected to the universe around us? *Wise Choices* promotes healthy, optimal aging. This pioneering book is practical, informed, realistic, challenging, and collaborative. Use it for life planning, as an encyclopedia of information you really need to know, for health planning, as a networking source, and for financial planning."
  —Frederic M. Hudson, PhD, author of *Life Launch: A Passionate Guide to the Rest of Your Life*

"*Wise Choices Beyond Midlife* is available to mature women for use in planning for their later lives in sound, secure, and interesting ways. This interdisciplinary approach to the challenges of aging assists the older woman in making realistic plans to lead healthier and more satisfying lives now and in the future."
  —Carol H. Tice, MEd, president, Lifespan Resources, Inc.

"*Wise Choices* is courageous in its willingness to face all the challenging daily realities that come with age and that are usually swept aside. This book will be a good companion to all who take it up—and I hope that will be a great many readers. They will find it to be a testament to hope."
  —Theodore Roszak, author of *The Making of a Counter Culture* and *The Memoirs of Elizabeth Frankenstein*

"Comprehensive, full of practical resources, clearly written, deep with experience and compassion. Although primarily intended for women over sixty, it is a must-read book for women of all ages who want to chart their own life journey with confidence, courage, and joy."
  —Barrie Robinson, MSSW, School of Social Welfare, University of California at Berkeley

D1018180

"*Wise Choices* is more than a well-written, comprehensive resource and workbook; it offers comfort and good advice with suggestions that can lead the reader (both men and women in their fifties and sixties) to meaningful and fulfilling future plans. In the complicated world of the 1990s with the myriad of multidimensional problems many people often face, *Wise Choices* proposes some clear thinking resolutions of many personal issues. The concepts related to decision making, work, time, and retirement are exceptionally well-delineated."

> —Barbara R. Ginsberg, EdD, executive director, My Turn Program, Kingsborough Community College, The City University of New York and editorial board chair, The Older Learner, American Society on Aging

"*Wise Choices Beyond Midlife* is one of the first 'do it yourself' guides on aging for women. Women are living longer and yet are unprepared for their later years. *Wise Choices* provides a foundation for decision making—offering advice from health to finances—in a simple, direct manner with easy-to-use worksheets and up-to-date resource guides. Readable and usable, I believe midlife women will benefit from this book."

> —Carroll L. Estes, PhD, director, Institute for Health and Aging, University of California at San Francisco

WISE CHOICES BEYOND MIDLIFE

Women Mapping the Journey Ahead

Lucy Scott, PhD
with Kerstin Joslyn Schremp, PhD,
Betty Soldz, BSW, and Barbara Weiss, MSW

Papier-Mache Press

WATSONVILLE, CA

01 00 99 98 97   5 4 3 2 1

ISBN: 1-57601-051-1 Softcover

Design and composition by Ursula Brookbank
Copyedited by Kim Van Dyke
Proofread by Sangeet Duchane
Indexed by Roberta Shepard
Authors' photograph by Irv Kermish
Manufactured by Malloy Lithographing, Inc.

Library of Congress Cataloging-in-Publication Data

Scott, Lucy, 1928–
    Wise choices beyond midlife: women mapping the journey ahead / Lucy Scott
with Kerstin Joslyn Schremp, Betty Soldz, and Barbara Weiss.
      p. cm.
    Includes bibliographical references and index.
    ISBN 1-57601-051-1 (alk. paper)
      1. Aged women—United States—Psychology. 2. Aged women—Health and
hygiene—United States. 3. Aged women—United States—Life skills guides. I. Title.
HQ1064.U5S394   1997
305.26—dc21   97-11355
                                            CIP

DEDICATION
To our husbands, David, Jim, Milton, and Irv,
and our families—with gratitude for their inspiration,
support, and reassurance.

CONTENTS

FOREWORD

TISH SOMMERS WAS THE founder and first president of the Older Women's League (OWL). She believed strongly that as women we must take action to better our lives and fight for improved access to health care, increased financial independence, and greater control of our days until their end. The truth of her principles still rings loudly today.

The issues that motivated Tish and the women who worked with her led to the development of a creative educational tool known as Wingspan. Thousands of women have successfully used the Wingspan model to better their quality of life as they age.

The Wingspan model is as important today as it was seventeen years ago at OWL's founding. Indeed, many of the same concerns are still with us.

Women are still the primary caregivers in our society; 75 percent of us will spend some time in our lives caring for children, sick spouses, or ailing parents. The aging of our society has created a sandwich generation. As women live longer and delay childbearing, those in midlife increasingly care simultaneously for their children and for their mothers and grandmothers. Women today spend an average of eleven years in a caregiving role away from the workforce, eleven years that we are not paying into Social Security or vesting in pensions.

Women have fought for and won a chance at higher rungs on the employment ladder, but we still earn only 72 percent of what men earn for equal jobs. This means even less money coming our way for retirement.

And we still fight for access to quality health care for all women.

Universal access is our call to action.

Wise Choices Beyond Midlife: Women Mapping the Journey Ahead is an integrated guide of practical ideas and resources that addresses these issues. The knowledge within these pages is intended to help women choose and change their life directions. Changing directions in life need not be tragic, but our decisions will require wisdom and courage. Wisdom is the ability to apply knowledge well. Courage is the will to apply knowledge now.

The authors of *Wise Choices Beyond Midlife: Women Mapping the Journey Ahead* have done a wonderful thing in writing a book that we can read, carry with us, and share with our neighbors, friends, and daughters. Don't pass sixty without it!

Wisdom brought this book to fruition.

Those with courage will read this book; those with wisdom and courage will implement what they learn here.

Now . . . let the journey begin.

—Johnetta Marshall, President, Older Women's League

PREFACE

IT ALL STARTED WHEN we first came together, eight women over sixty, to talk about making our way through aging. Our intention was to meet six times to discuss Betty Friedan's book, *The Fountain of Age*, then go our separate ways. The idea to form this group was born from what we later discovered to be a shared longing: to find other women who speak the common language of having lived at least six decades. As each monthly meeting ended with our setting another meeting date, it became clear that our conversations expressed a deeper need to speak, listen, learn, and do something about our own experiences of aging. So what was meant to be a book discussion took on a life of its own, stretched to two years, and launched a book.

As our discussions continued, we explored and reviewed many books, newsletters, conference agendas, and publications about women and about aging. What we found emphasized the problems of aging, focused narrowly on one topic or another, or exhorted us to remake ourselves in order to live happily ever after. We searched for helpful ideas and explanations in the literature of our own professions: gerontology, psychology, education, sociology, social work, and community activism. Some of what we found was useful, but neither the academically based research nor the personal stories were enough. We felt strongly that, since old age can only be avoided by dying young, the real question, "Where do we go from here with our life?" was still unexplained. We valiantly plunged on in our discussions, and four of us became The Book Group.

During the researching and writing of this book we listened to each other, debated our differences, and tried to find the words to honor our diversity yet remain true to the central themes of our own individual life experiences. There is something about collaborating with a group on any task that colors its product and makes the process a true adventure.

What came through repeatedly in our discussions and those of the larger group of women over sixty were the undefined and unexpected strengths, skills, courage, and creativity we bring to this stage of life. The shadow side of aging was also present in our conversations: fears, worries, and the practical problems faced every day— money, health, husbands, families—and the hunger and disappointments in our hearts. Our voices merged into this book.

The four of us have been shaped by composite careers and by a kaleidoscope of education and life experiences. Now elderhood has arrived and, like so many other women, we have been appalled to discover how little is actually known about these stages of a woman's life. Our investment in this topic reflects what matters to us now and what we care about. It expresses our interest, curiosity, and passionate desire to understand and find answers to the puzzling questions women face in the last decades of life, and to communicate this to others in ways that may encourage them to see the potential in their later years.

The goal of writing a definitive book about women and aging demands confidence, discipline, commitment, and possibly a component of arrogance. But our activism won out. We are proud that we speak, as women beyond sixty, to other women. Our own narratives are behind every statistic and statement. We are also pleased that we have written from the diversity of our life stories, with sensitivity and respect for the complexity and uniqueness of many women's lives.

ACKNOWLEDGMENTS

WE ARE ESPECIALLY INDEBTED to the openhearted women in our Elder Women's Group who met together once a month for over two years: Marge Chapman, Fran Glibas, Edith Kasin, Simone Klugman, Shirley Mastrangeli, and Elizabeth Zackheim. Our conversations inspired and shaped this book. Special thanks go to Harriet Renaud, who offered her wise advice and support to this writing adventure.

We would also like to express our appreciation and gratitude to the many clients and colleagues whose strengths and concerns have contributed to our understanding of women's lives. The names of those who have influenced us would form a very long list.

The pioneering work of Tish Sommers and Laurie Shields and the Older Women's League provided us with a solid foundation.

Janet Van Deusen, program manager of the Health Insurance Counseling and Advocacy Program of Alameda County, deserves special thanks for her assistance to Betty Soldz.

And finally, we thank our editor, Shirley Coe, who guided us in completing this journey.

Introduction

THIS BOOK IS ABOUT life beyond sixty for women. It is intended to inform, reassure, inspire, and empower women to live their lives beyond sixty with dignity, courage, and as much joy, satisfaction, and contentment as possible. We don't believe a dream such as this comes true automatically with age, but depends for the most part on how actively we manage our lives by meeting and solving the challenges we face as older women.

This is not a book about "them," but about us: women speaking to other women. For this reason we want to first emphasize our diversity, then the issues that unite us.

Elder Women: Defined and Undefined

Despite the fact that "elderly" can entail thirty or more years, the 24 million women who are over sixty are often described generically. In reality, we represent many subgroups and subcultures with respect to age, marital status, health, income, ethnicity, sexual orientation, housing, educational background, and values. This diverse population includes those who continue to work for pay as respected and productive contributors to society; those who may never have worked for pay and still depend on families for protection and support; those who are active caretakers of husbands, families, or grandchildren; and those who are married, divorced, widowed, or have always been single—heterosexual or lesbian, rich or poor, healthy or frail, active or inactive, energized or depressed and lonely. There is not just one old woman, but many.

In fact, we become less like each other as we age. Labels such as "senior citizen," "elder," "golden-ager," or merely "old" describe us no more accurately than "child" or "adult" describes other age groups. However, some qualities and life issues are consistently present in older women. These themes and the questions they suggest form the core of this book.

Eight Life-Changing Challenges

1. How can I maintain a satisfying and dignified life?

A serious question for anyone, but for women this question has special meaning because life beyond sixty is more different now than before. Reasons for our uncertainty about the future are examined in chapter one within the context of the personal, social, and historic uniqueness of becoming an elder woman in the closing years of this century.

2. What can I do to prevent or manage health problems?

Health problems and debilitating physical deterioration top the list of worries for older women. Longer lives increase the risk of illness, chronic disease, and physical disability. The good news, however, is that we can take an active role in caring for ourselves and managing the health care system to support our own healthy aging. Chapter two contains information, support, and strategies to do this.

3. How can I support myself?

A financially secure old age is far from automatic for women. There are wide economic differences among women of all ages, but older women are especially vulnerable to shrinking financial resources. Reasons for this vulnerability form the financial facts of life for older women. A guide to understanding these issues and the problems they engender, and a plan for actively and courageously facing them, is the focus of chapter three.

4. What are my choices about where I live?

Where we live and with whom is a question close to the hearts and pocketbooks of older women. Choices about housing involve much more than just practical financial and safety issues. Health, convenience, and accessibility to essential services are factors we face when we are forced to balance independence with increasing dependence. Chapter four discusses these issues and offers practical alternatives for their solution.

5. How can I spend my time in a meaningful way?

What can older women do with the rest of our lives? What should we do? Decisions about paid and unpaid work, and what we now call leisure, have special consequences and implications for women. The roles of our own expectations—and those of our friends, families, and culture—in how we choose to spend our time are critical and complex. Chapter five examines retirement and life beyond, with an emphasis on searching for ways to enrich, fulfill, and create satisfaction in the later decades of life.

6. How can I manage caretaking for others?

It is a rare woman who does not care for a sick or aging husband, sibling, partner, or other family member in her later years. The satisfaction of giving care and the downside of guilt, exhaustion, anger, isolation, helplessness, and stress are reviewed in chapter six, which is a practical guide for assessing and managing caregiving, with suggestions for finding and using support services.

7. How can I get care for myself if I need it?

In the past, daughters were expected to be the prime caregivers of their parents. Due to changes in societal dynamics, most daughters are no longer available for this role. Most women also outlive their spouses or have husbands who are unable to provide care. Chapter seven examines the problems women have in obtaining care in their old age. Care options and how to pay for them, especially for women with limited incomes, are discussed and encouragement is offered to plan ahead in order to maintain control of one's health and life.

8. *How can I prepare for dying and death?*
Facing our own death and that of others without morbidly and negatively obsessing over it is the ultimate life challenge. The final chapter of this book introduces a philosophical and practical view of preparing for the end of life. As our own time left to live becomes a precious commodity to be savored and appreciated, we can actively consider both the practical and emotional issues of dying. Our hope is that by facing the challenge of death, we can die with life.

We're All One Piece
Integration and wholeness are underlying themes of this book. Each chapter is a thread in the tapestry of life for women over sixty. We weave each issue in these chapters into an interdependent, coherent whole. It seems clear that managing our money and understanding health insurance or housing options are necessary, but not sufficient, to sustain us or answer the deeper questions in our hearts.

The conceptual base for this approach was Wingspan, a comprehensive program for older women first conceived by Tish Sommers, then president of the Older Women's League. Wingspan consisted of a series of workshops and workbooks based on seven issues identified in a national survey conducted by the Older Women's League in the early 1980s. It was evident even then that the challenges older women face are extraordinarily complex, intertwined, and enduring.

How to Use This Book
So here it is: a book to illuminate the journey ahead. We propose that aging is not a single event, but a journey full of adventure and surprises. However, planning for the future unquestionably strengthens our sense of power over our lives. Planning also gives us some

understanding about what we can and can't control. Reasonable planning is enriching and empowering; obsessive planning for every unknown emergency ahead is not helpful in our search for a healthy life for ourselves and those we care about. Anyway, life sometimes deals us a wild card!

This book is designed as a road map into new territory; it is a resource for older women, their families, and those who care about them. It may be used by an individual, a family, an informal group or women's organization, and in settings such as churches, community centers, and schools.

The people who open this book will do so for many reasons: to reassure themselves that their life is in order, to learn how to ensure a better future for themselves, or to answer a concern about a personal problem. Think of this book as a smorgasbord of ideas, information, and strategies—then use the combination most helpful to you. The self-assessment worksheets, activities, planning guides, and resource lists are intended to encourage you to become a more informed and empowered elder person, and to take responsibility for your own life by:

+ assessing personal strengths and challenges
+ becoming more informed about common life concerns
+ understanding and appreciating your uniqueness
+ learning how to find, evaluate, and use personal support services from families, friends, and community resources
+ planning to take action to maintain and improve your life

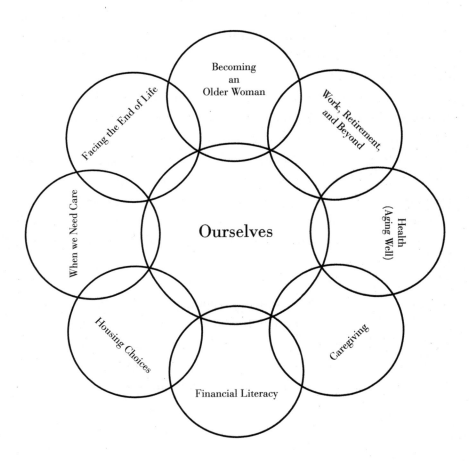

WISE CHOICES
BEYOND MIDLIFE

Women Mapping the Journey Ahead

Chapter One

BECOMING AN ELDER WOMAN:
Where Do I Go from Here?

Now there is time to tell the story
—time to invent the new one.
—Marilyn Zuckerman

THERE COMES A TIME in every woman's life when we turn a cor-
ner and the "golden years" stretch out beyond us. "You are here"
indicates the arrow on our life map, but where do we go from here?
Will the future be a period of serenity and fulfilled dreams as we go
gently into that dark night, cared for and respected by those we love,
or will it be shadowed by our frailty, dependence, loneliness, neglect?

In so many ways, life after sixty for women is unknown territory,
full of promises, surprises, contradictions, and dilemmas. But how
could we expect to be prepared for a time of life (ten, twenty, thirty,
or more years) for which there are few maps, models, or guides?

Books on childhood, adolescence, marriage, divorce, motherhood,
nonmotherhood, singlehood, midlife, and menopause crowd libraries
and bookstores. But where are the books that seriously approach life
after sixty as it occurs to real women? There is no shortage of books
written about us as elderly bodies with physical or mental illnesses or
advice on how to invest a retirement nest egg, how to choose a retire-

ment home, or how to achieve postmenopausal zest. However, books addressed to us as whole people facing and living with the real problems and joys of aging are rarely seen, or at best are squeezed between *Senior Adventures Abroad* or *Golden Opportunities* on bookstore shelves. Gail Sheehy's recent book describing the new passages of adult life devotes only five out of nearly five hundred pages to the seventies and beyond. Lacking from the pages of most books about elder women are the voices of elder women speaking about our own lives. Where is the guidebook we need for life ahead?

It is no wonder that we enter this new territory tentatively, experimenting with a future that is undefined. The reasons for our uncertainty are all around us. Some come from within ourselves, but others are from the historical moment in which we live. Our culture has had little experience with older, healthy, active women, who are increasing in our population. Even the women's movement has only recently begun to publicly recognize the voices and needs of older women.

THE CONTEXT OF OUR JOURNEY: FROM THERE TO HERE

We could say, in retrospect, that all of our lives have led us inevitably and fatefully to this point. After all, we have traveled a long road—six, seven, eight, or nine decades—to get here. Born early in this century, we have lived on the crest of waves of change, arriving at succeeding life stages just before anybody knew quite what to do next. As we try to understand the challenges of our remaining years, it is reassuring to remember that choices we make about our future not only reflect our place in history, but our uniqueness as women. Robert Butler, former head of the National Institute of Aging, has said, "Because women are, in fact, the great majority of the old, the problems of age are really women's problems."

It is, of course, easier to name the problems than to find personal solutions to them. Worries about poor health, financial dependence, housing changes, caregiving, loneliness, loss of family and friends, and approaching death are not new for older people. But the context in which we search for solutions is new. It is a reflection of our uncertainty about our time left to live, the probability that we'll be single, the pressures of ageism, lessons from our past, our lack of role models, our diversity, and of new messages about how to grow old with "political correctness."

It's About Time

In 1900, when many of our mothers were born, life expectancy for women was forty-eight years. Women barely lived long enough to see all their children leave home. Old age for women began at what we now regard as vigorous midlife, and a rocking chair on the porch symbolized life ahead.

Times have changed. We are living longer than ever before, and our numbers are growing. Twenty-four million of us are now over sixty, and we greatly outnumber men in this age group. Even though our life span as a group is reduced by decreasing health, an inadequate income, lack of education, and being a member of a minority group, the potential for a longer life is greater than ever before. For the first time in history, old age, for women, can easily span thirty years. The ordinary woman who reaches sixty-five can fully expect to continue living for twenty or more years. These years are often unanticipated, unplanned for, and hold no guarantee of happiness. No matter where we fit on the statistical curve of probability, we represent a remarkable demographic shift in life-span potential.

Being Single

Not only can we expect to live longer than ever before, but we are likely to live at least some of those extra years alone. Numbers tell the story. Since women statistically outlive men and are often younger than their mates, most women over sixty-five are single and live alone. Eighty-five percent of wives outlive their husbands (the reverse is true for men). More than nine million elderly Americans live alone; 78 percent of them are women. The longer we live, the greater chance we have of being single. The U.S. Census Bureau's 1996 Current Population Report states that 48.6 percent of women sixty-five and older were widowed, and only 10.5 percent of those over eighty-five were married. Among African-American older women, the proportion is even higher, with 82.6 percent of those over seventy-five being widows. An increasing number of women over sixty are also single because they never married or were divorced.

These numbers have importation implications for women. Most older women will be faced with needing to take charge of and shape their own lives. Reinventing oneself as a single woman is a formidable challenge. The greatest hurdle may be that of building and maintaining a network of friends who can provide mutual help, companionship, and support. Reshaping existing relationships with family and friends can be a daunting task in a couple-oriented social network.

It would be a mistake to conclude, however, that life as a single woman must be an altogether negative experience. Many women find an unexpected release of creativity and inner peace in solitude and independence; a time when the possibilities for becoming oneself unfold.

From Lifetime Caretaking to Choice

We have lived in a time of profound changes in attitudes and expectations regarding women's roles. When we were very young, we may have imagined life like that of our mothers, defined by being a good wife and mother and emerging into old age as our grandmothers had—tolerated or respected, but cared for by our families until death. We expected our lives to be shaped by our relationship to our families. Even diagrams of the family life cycle were divided into neatly defined pie-shaped wedges labeled "childhood," "marriage and motherhood," "empty nest," and "old age."

We had no choice regarding these roles, something now taken for granted by young women. Lifetime caring for others was predetermined. Educational opportunity, job choice, and finding a husband were confined to early adulthood. But our generation entered the stage of adulthood at a time in history that has required a new script. Some social and historical influences have been subtle, some profoundly life changing: an economic depression; two major wars; revolutions in the structure and shape of our families; evolving attitudes toward roles for men, women, and children; dramatic increases in the size, diversity, and mobility of our population; the women's movement; and government programs have intervened in our lives. Social Security, Medicare, Elderhostels, and Sun City were, of course, unknown to our grandmothers.

As we struggled to remake ourselves in response to these social upheavals, most of us can describe our lives as having been a series of challenges, public and private. Who among us cannot recall growing up with the expectation that we could somehow choose the right husband, become a Dr. Spock super mother, and live happily ever after? Our formative years were clearly marked by messages such as "Something from the oven says loving." We have even been labeled the Silent Generation.

Those of us who have survived these turbulent decades may feel that we lived our lives in the best of times, when choices were simpler, but there is no doubt that we have been challenged to repeatedly redefine ourselves as we mothered hippies, baby boomers, yuppies, and stepchildren; divorced and remarried; returned to school; entered and reentered the workforce; retired; and became widows and grandmothers. Now, old age appears to be yet another life stage demanding that we regroup once again for the life we have left to live. Where are the role models we need?

From Betty Crocker to the Golden Girls

I keep looking for someone that looks like me on prime time. In our youth we saw visual images that acknowledged and honored our existence: Father Knows Best, Betty Crocker, and Lana Turner were there to emulate. We have occasionally seen the honored, aging faces of Katherine Hepburn, Georgia O'Keeffe, Maggie Kuhn, Margaret Mead, Maya Angelou, or an admired grandmother. But beyond the rare older woman represented by television's The Golden Girls or Angela Lansbury in Murder She Wrote, our images as elder women on television are missing, or are negative and devaluing, exhibiting qualities of childishness, frailty, or needing male protection.

With a few rare exceptions, older women remain nearly invisible in American films. Roles in which women over sixty have a career or are working are rare, despite the fact that 15 percent of real-world women age sixty and over are in the labor force.

The opposite of these negative images often occur in magazines designed for older or mature readers, portraying us as active, happy, thin, well-dressed, wrinkle-free shoppers. "I'm not going to age gracefully; I'm going to fight it every step of the way," reads the caption in a recent ad campaign for face cream. We seem to have entered a new category of smiling consumers, often seen in magazine photographs standing beside a handsome, white-haired man who is obviously competent, healthy, financially secure, and concerned about our happiness. Neither the frail, dependent older woman nor the active, smiling shopper stereotype reflect the reality of our daily lives. And the media's new message can chip away our sense of self-esteem.

The Mythology of the Elderly Olympics

We are being urged to become politically correct about aging—anything is possible. The elderly Olympics are just ahead. Get Up and Go!, a personal magazine for older women, encourages us to keep looking young by considering plastic surgery. We are surrounded by slogans attempting to pump up our enthusiasm for aging: start a new business, age productively, challenge our brains, exercise, eat only low-fat foods, take estrogen to preserve our health, apply wrinkle creams, travel, revive our sexual passions, and learn to manage our money. The value of these goals and the reward that they imply is undoubtedly positive and may even energize us, but expecting ever more of ourselves in the race to optimal aging is a choice, not a necessity.

Labels such as Sheehy's Serene Sixties, Sage Seventies, Uninhibited Eighties, Noble Nineties, and Celebratory Centenarians may be inspiring, but do they really inform and empower us to live our lives as elder women, or do they merely encourage new stereotypes to contain us? Can we still find respect and support for contentment, tolerance, and reflection or for being at peace with ourselves, our friends, our families, and the world? Can we still find the courage to be ourselves and to honor our diversity, achieving a gold medal for a life well-lived? The answers and the perspective of this book, is yes. However, there are contradictions to face in our journey.

Contradictions: A Glass Half Full or Half Empty?

This is a tricky business, becoming older, because contradictions of both promise and fear shadow us. When we think of the benefits and joys of having achieved this "ripe old age" of sixty, seventy, eighty, ninety, or more, we may smile in satisfaction and count our blessings. We do tend to be better-educated, healthier, and more autonomous than women of former generations. But for every entry in the positive column of the ledger, most of us can also see a shadow side.

Our passage into aging usually begins when we experience some marker event, such as a birthday, retirement, health problem, or loss of someone close to us. Expressions of relief, dismay, and uncertainty betray our feelings: "The first time I was offered a senior discount at the movie theater I felt insulted, but then I began to ask myself—

am I really a senior citizen now?" "For me, my sixtieth birthday seemed a real milestone. I didn't want a public celebration. It just seemed the beginning of the end." "I was delighted to retire at sixty-five. I thought—at last, I won't have to set the alarm every morning. I can read all the books I want."

What did we expect old age to be? More of the same? A reward for a life well-lived? Gardening, good works, and grandmothering?

FACING CHANGES

The common theme confronting us as we make our way through the landscape of aging is the probability that we will face changes in all the major areas of our life. Changes in ourselves, our families, and the communities in which we live are predictable. These form the heart of this book and are discussed in other chapters. The only way to avoid change is to die before it happens. Predicting the timing and the extent of life changes is, of course, impossible, except for the unarguable fact that our life is limited, and the older we are, the closer we are to death. Caring for our bodies, our minds, and our souls with this certainty is not easy, but looking within ourselves is a place to begin.

Our Personal Response Spectrum

Surely, one size does not fit all in predicting how we will meet the challenges ahead. For every change or turning point in our lives, we meet and respond to the challenge in our unique way. Wisdom, courage, survival skills, integrity, and resilience are balanced by feelings of self-doubt, anxiety, depression, despair, loneliness, bitterness, and vulnerability. *If my life goes on too long, I don't want my family to have to take care of me. I worry about being alone and being vulnerable, even walking in my neighborhood. I'm scared of growing old alone. I just get tired of having to take care of my ninety-three-year-old mother-in-law. I never thought I would be doing this in my own old age. I worry about running out of money. My current nightmare is becoming sick and helpless. People I know are dying. Am I next? Giving up my car keys is my worst nightmare.*

Recognizing Our Strengths

What's good about being an elder woman? Where do we look for our strengths? Aging has a way of encouraging growth of the best in us.

A place to begin is to recognize and appreciate the lessons we have learned in the past and build on them. Friedan names these "the strengths that have no name." Aside from the unexpected events over which we have no control (serious illness, accidents, death of those we love, financial losses, or earthquakes, fires, and floods), it is our psychological fitness, defined by Robert Butler as our social and personal fitness, that most likely determines the quality of our lives beyond sixty.

As elders, we can tap and nourish the wisdom of aging. Wisdom, by definition, is simply the common sense that has always been associated with older women. In past ages, old women were looked on as wise guardians of life's entrances and exits. Wisdom also implies qualities gained slowly, and often painfully over many years of life. We can draw upon this store of wisdom and apply it to choices that confront us now. We say, "I don't need to do that anymore; I've done that already and I know it doesn't work for me." Wisdom is like money in the bank for us. It represents integrity, integration, balance, self-mastery, serenity, self-confidence, and compassion.

To respect and honor these qualities in ourselves does not imply, however, a Pollyanna "Everything-will-be-all-right-if-I-just-smile-or-take-a-nap" attitude. There is a clear distinction between passivity and peacefulness. Women over sixty do face genuine problems, which deserve our attention and action.

Wisdom is strengthened by another quality we share: simply, the skill of survival, the certainty we have acquired that no matter what happens, we can find the strength within ourselves to work it out or to make hard choices. The term *resilience*, now being used in psychological literature, describes this quality of survival as the ability to adapt to a changing environment while remaining connected to the past. For elder women, the word may be new, but the experience is not. Learning to survive, even thrive, in the face of crises has formed the major unifying theme of our lives. Another way to empower ourselves to cope with changes is to nurture our belief in our own capability and competence. Feeling empowered rather than powerless in the face of problems strengthens us. Learning to cope with changes and transitions is not new, but an already acquired skill we can draw on.

The ability to shift our attitudes and priorities when life circumstances demand a change can make the difference between despair and aging well. For example, joy in living may be found in unexpected places. *My joy now is in reading a story to my grandson. I love to see his little face light up. When I see the sun in the morning, I am truly happy. To read in the afternoon is my well-earned luxury.* These expressions have little connection with the "keep-busy" vision of aging. But the joy of age is in finding what truly nourishes the mind, heart, and spirit. Pursuing our individual dreams now requires the same adaptations, resilience, creativity, and courage as did challenges in our earlier years.

Another strength we acquire as elders is the ability to make peace with ourselves and those around us, to let go of what didn't happen and what probably won't happen now. Reaching for our own truth becomes more important than before. We ask ourselves questions such as, "What has my life been about, how will I be remembered, and what is worth doing now?" Erik Erikson, in his model of eight life stages, suggested that the eighth and final stage of adult development is a struggle between integrity and despair. If integrity, as he suggested, implies the capacity and serenity to accept one's life history as something that had to be, then bringing all the parts of one's life into harmony is our task in aging.

Changes in Our Bodies and Ourselves

Because we live in a culture in which youth, thinness, physical vitality, and beauty are synonymous with desirability and acceptability, older women find it difficult to feel comfortable about the inevitable physical effects of aging. How can we believe we are only as old as we feel when we are absent from the covers of magazines and advertisements for fashion and beauty?

When we look in the mirror and wonder whatever happened to the body and face of our youth, we are not simply questioning the acceptability of our size and shape. We are mourning the loss of our value as an acceptable woman. Body image is an important part of our self-concept, an influence not only on the way we think of ourselves, but also on our feelings of competence and the value of our identity. Who among us has not looked carefully into the mirror as we tried to decide whether to attend a school reunion?

We should, of course, expect to change in shape and appearance as we age. We gain weight and get wrinkled skin and grey hair. We even use hearing aids, canes, or walkers that lead to restrictions in our social activities. By acknowledging these changes instead of feeling shame and guilt for no longer appearing "young," we can nourish our feelings of pride and value ourselves for who we are, not who we are not.

FAMILY AFFAIRS: JOYS AND SORROWS

Our lives have been defined largely by our family roles and responsibilities. Concern for these relationships has been a central theme in our lives, sometimes described as the cornerstone of female development. We have all been shaped by being first daughters, then for some wives, mothers, and grandmothers. Beyond sixty, we can anticipate changes in family relationships and attachments, often related to the loss of family members, our need to give care, or the need to be cared for ourselves.

The romanticized view of the golden years, in which couples see themselves growing old side by side, is not always realized. Age more often brings the complications of retirement and financial worries, chronic illness and frailty, changing sex roles, and dependence. Women may be especially susceptible to these adjustments when they feel responsible for their spouse's happiness and well-being as well as their own. Having time to spend together can be enormously satisfying and a source of real mutual support or be shadowed by conflict and anxiety.

For those of us who have raised families, our caregiving role may expand to include unexpected layers. Because of her extended life span, it is not unusual for an older woman to be involved with the care of her parents, her spouse, her children, and her grandchildren.

Becoming a Grandmother

For most women, becoming a grandmother is an exciting and heart-warming experience. Traditionally, the wisdom of the older woman has been concentrated in the role of grandmother, but it is somewhat of a paradox that, in recent years, the role has become less clear. Today's grandmothers range in age from forty to over a hundred, their grandchildren from newborns to retirees. The years spent as a grand-mother has expanded along with our life span. As more of our daughters endeavor to balance full-time work with caring for their children and face repeated child-care crises, our attention and concern as grandmothers has become more critical to family stability.

The U.S. Census reports that about 3.4 million children live in households headed by one or both grandparents.

Grandmothers often experience considerable conflict between their desire to be independent and live their own lives, and their desire to be responsive to their children's needs for help with young children. The image of the grey-haired cookie-baker rarely fits today's physically active and socially involved grandmother. Most grandmothers see their role as being emotionally close to their grandchildren, without feeling responsible for regular child care. Others enjoy and feel responsible for taking a major role in the care of grandchildren.

Even when time spent with grandchildren is limited, often because families live far away, we can provide a reliable anchor in a child's life. By being an understanding listener, offering advice as a cautious and wise guardian and mentor, and keeping in touch by mail or by phone, we can play an important and special role.

When Things Go Wrong in Families

Family relationships are rarely totally wonderful, satisfying, and loving. Even families with warm, caring, and healthy feelings for each other do not have them all the time. Unfortunately, aging often increases our need for support and assistance. As our physical energies diminish, our families often face the dilemma of taking over the management of our lives. When we are forced to seek increasing assistance from our families with problems concerning money, health, and frailty, family members can feel overwhelmed with the responsibility for our care and confused about "what to do about Mother."

Family relationships can become emotionally charged, manipulative, and even abusive. An aging parent may dominate, intimidate, or manipulate an adult child or other family member, or a younger family member may ignore or mistreat an aging parent. The solutions to these problems can be emotionally wrenching for everyone involved and often bring disappointments, failed expectations, and conflicts. Finding ways to reconcile our hurts, our disagreements, and our love for each other requires courage, honesty, and sometimes help from someone outside the family. No one deserves to live in fear. Later chapters of this book offer helpful suggestions for assessing and managing family problems with finances, health, housing, caregiving, receiving care, and preparing for death.

COMPOSING THE FUTURE

There is a wise saying that tells us to live our lives forward, since going backward in time is not possible (even with virtual imaging). It may be too late to wonder who we're going to be when we grow up, but not too late to plan for the future, to make important personal changes, or to have an impact on the world around us.

Writer May Sarton, in *At Seventy, A Journal*, raises and answers the question: "Why is it good to be old? Because I am more myself than I have ever been." If we do become more of who we already are as we age, then our challenge is to emphasize the best parts of ourselves and accept the worst. Nothing makes us grow old as fast as hardening of the heart, which has little to do with dependence on money, position, education, or power. None of us is a superwoman. We don't all need to do illustrious deeds; yet all of us can dream, think, learn, plan, and do something to enhance the quality of our lives. How we speak to each other, how we spend our time, how we care for others and ourselves—all of these express who we are and what we value. When fears panic us and problems seem insurmountable, we tend to blame ourselves and feel inadequate, but we can only do our best. We can even choose what we want to leave undone.

Choice and Change

Choice and change are familiar words to us—as are resistance, helplessness, uncertainty, and powerlessness. But resistance is a normal and predictable companion of change. It is not something to ignore or avoid, but something to recognize and acknowledge. Despair, the belief that time is too short or that we are powerless to change anything in our lives, can fall across our path as a shadow. When we find ourselves continuing to do, say, or think these things that keep us from getting what we say we want, it is time for a new strategy. If the mountain seems to be formidable, go around it. Even asking for help is self-affirming. One of the meanings of wisdom is knowing that we can still reorder what is important to us, become more informed, and take action to become the kind of older woman we want to be.

Feeling Connected

Feeling connected by social ties or networks has a direct positive effect on mortality and health. The benefits of social networks can come from families, groups of friends, groups sponsored by community organizations, or churches. Even computer-based networks are now being accessed by elders to provide social and informational interaction and support.

It is no accident that we are currently seeing a revival of interest in wise-woman groups. Many of the ideas in this book originated in such a group—a group of eight women over sixty who came together to find our voices, to listen to each other, to inspire, inform, empower, support, and challenge each other, as we searched for our way through the frontier of our aging. We have much to learn from each other and little time to waste. We don't need to wait for legislation or a government grant to do this. It takes only one woman and a telephone to begin.

The value and power of small circles of women has been well-documented throughout history. Informal support groups become even more essential when external authority provides conflicting messages for the problems and questions central to our lives. It is time, once again, to revive and nourish the sharing of the wisdom of elder women. We long to hear from each other; to give and receive support.

Shaping Our Future

It is remarkably interesting to be old—looking out at the world we're moving away from—but we need a dream as well as a memory. The question we face now is "What do I want to be remembered for?" The message here is that no path is hard or easy. A certain amount of anxiety and risk is part of any choice. It may be hard to give up the idea that there is a ready-made blueprint for our lives, but exploring life ahead is worth the risk.

To a large degree, we write our own internal scripts and shape our own futures. In order to do this, we need to validate our experience and find the information, courage, and strength to create our own map for the future. As Marcel Proust suggests:"The real voyage of discovery consists not in seeking new landscapes, but in having new eyes."

It is time to take stock, to appreciate what we know, and to design the journey ahead. This book is devoted to inspiring, informing, and empowering you to do this. The following chapters are designed as a map of exploration for the woman who wants to maintain a satisfying and dignified life beyond sixty. They provide information and offer suggestions for answering these seven vital questions:

* What can I do to prevent or manage health problems?

* How can I support myself?

* What are my choices about where I live?

* How can I spend my time in a meaningful way?

* How can I manage caretaking for others?

* How can I get care for myself if I need it?

* How can I prepare for dying and death?

Chapter Two

HEALTHY AGING:
Taking Stock and Taking Action

Why is it that time does not stop
That to stay well and to feel well
Even when we're not
Becomes a way of life?
—Anonymous

HEALTH IS AT THE top of our list of concerns as we age. Whether we are in good health and able to live a vital, active life, or whether chronic illness and physical problems shadow us, our bodies remind us of the increasing vulnerability that accompanies aging.

We can expect much longer life spans than either our mothers or most men, but we also know in our hearts that an acute or chronic health problem can change our lives in a moment. Even though countless older women overcome the adversity of disease and continue to live highly productive lives, there is good reason to fear illness, pain, and reduced physical capacities. These often result in dependence, anxiety, immobility, and economic insecurity. As we grow older we become increasingly vulnerable to heart disease, cancer, osteoporosis, diabetes, arthritis, and Alzheimer's disease, sensory loss, incontinence, and depression. Even when we remain in good health during the thirty-plus potential years of life beyond sixty, the basic biology of aging brings us ever closer to dying and death.

There are, of course, increasing numbers of vital older women enjoying better health than ever before. Many chronic conditions are preventable, most are treatable, and all can be compensated for to some extent. New attitudes about wellness and the value of self-care are encouraging women to take an active role in preventing illness, in adapting to physical problems as they occur, and in striving to age well.

Even though we may incur serious illnesses, the quality of our everyday life cannot be automatically determined from the names of the diseases we have, but more by our ability to care for ourselves or to enlist the kind of support and assistance we need. How we respond to and compensate for physical problems—how our daily life is affected—depends on many of the factors discussed in the chapters of this book. For example, an eighty-year-old woman with hypertension, diabetes, and osteoarthritis might live alone, be an active community volunteer, or be a disabled resident of a skilled nursing facility, depending on her ability to care for herself or to enlist the kind of support she needs to maintain her activities.

AGING WELL—THE BIG PICTURE

A major thesis of this chapter is that health is a personal and social as well as a biological phenomenon. Aging well is not simply avoiding major illness, but rather implies that we maintain physical, social, and psychological fitness: a harmony of body, mind, and spirit. This goal involves much more than waiting until we are in pain to see a physician and hoping that there will be a magic treatment or medication to cure us. It suggests, instead, that we make better use of diet, exercise, and self-care, maximizing the knowledge we have, or finding a way to learn more, about our bodies. It also underscores the importance of finding accessible and affordable medical, social, and psychological resources. Unfortunately, Medicare reimburses acute care much more generously than preventive services. So the challenge of aging well is to assess our strengths as well as our problems, learn to prevent problems from becoming disabilities, and prevent disabilities from causing dependence, fear, and hopelessness.

For those of us who grew up depending on a man in a white coat to advise, prescribe for, and cure us, it is a challenge to move from passivity to having some control over the quality of our lives. Getting information to make decisions about medical treatment, or knowing how to find assistance to manage our lives in spite of a disabling physical problem, is a challenge. Our ability to be honest about our own strengths and weaknesses, to be committed to self-care, and to respond to problems with courage and determination increase our chances for aging well and preserving the quality of our lives. Our best investment is in our personal health portfolios.

COMMON HEALTH CONCERNS OF OLDER WOMEN

It is well-known that diseases such as heart disease, cancer, osteoporosis, diabetes, arthritis, and Alzheimer's disease are major threats to older women's health. Other impairments such as sensory loss, incontinence, or depression, and lifestyle abuses such as misuse of medications and drugs, malnutrition, inactivity, or smoking also profoundly affect our health. Some of these are life threatening, some contribute to more serious illness. They all affect significant numbers of older women. However, women can prevent, delay, or lessen the impact of these and other risk factors. The following section is not meant to be a laundry list of diseases, but is intended to help women make informed choices about their own care.

Heart Disease
One in three older women develop heart disease, the leading cause of hospitalization and death in women over sixty-five. Although many of

the risk factors associated with this deadly disease are controllable, the condition is often diagnosed late and many women are unaware of its symptoms and warning signs. Delayed diagnosis and treatment unnecessarily increase morbidity and mortality rates among women.

Heart disease is a general term covering all ailments of the heart. Cardiovascular disease is a broad term referring to disorders of the heart (cardio) and circulatory (vascular) system. This includes hypertension, atherosclerosis, stroke, rheumatic heart disease, and other disorders. Coronary artery disease refers to conditions that cause narrowing of the coronary arteries so that blood flow to the heart is reduced. Permanent damage to the heart muscle is called a heart attack (myocardial infarction).

Another serious condition related to atherosclerosis is a cerebral embolism (hemorrhage) or stroke. A stroke occurs when the flow of blood to an area of the brain is disrupted. In a cerebral embolism, a burst artery floods the brain tissue with blood. Heart disease and long-standing hypertension are major causes of strokes.

Risk factors that have been shown to have a significant impact on heart disease are: smoking, hypertension, high cholesterol, diabetes, obesity, stress, family history, and physical inactivity. Many of these can be reduced or managed by early detection and improved habits.

Early detection is especially important in identifying hypertension (elevated blood pressure), present in two-thirds of all women over sixty-five. It is estimated that only about half of women who are hypertensive know of their disease. Symptoms such as headaches or dizziness are often masked or attributed to other causes. The aim of treatment for coronary artery disease is to prevent the ultimate consequence of the disease process—heart attack or strokes.

Although healthy habits are no guarantee that we can prevent cardiovascular disease, it is evident from the list of these risk factors that early medical detection and monitoring of cholesterol and blood pressure is important in reducing risk. Equally important, however, is achieving and maintaining a lifestyle that eliminates smoking and includes a low-fat, low-cholesterol diet; moderate, regular exercise; and reduced stress.

Women should be aware of the early warning signs of heart attack—pressure or pain in the center of your chest lasting two minutes or more. This pain may spread to your arms, shoulders, neck, or jaw and can be accompanied by dizziness, fainting, sweating, or nausea.

The warning signs of stroke include: weakness or numbness in the face, arm, or leg on one side of your body; a severe, persistent headache; loss of speech or difficulty speaking; loss of vision; dizziness; or unsteadiness.

Recovery and rehabilitation from heart attacks and strokes include a variety of medications, surgery, exercise, and diet programs, as well as education, support groups, counseling, stress reduction, and speech and occupational therapy.

Cancer

The word "cancer" can stimulate a multitude of emotional responses, from fear and dread to denial and sadness. Almost every older woman has been touched by the loss of a loved one from cancer, or lives with the fear of a recurrence or the development of cancer in herself or a loved one. These fears are grounded in reality. Women over sixty-five are at high risk for developing cancer, and the risk grows with age.

Lung cancer kills more women than any other type of cancer. The risk of developing breast cancer is one in seventeen for women by age sixty-five; this risk increases to one in nine by age eighty-five. About one-third of all women with breast cancer will die of the disease. In addition to lung and breast cancer, women are also at risk for developing cancer of the colon or rectum, cervix, or uterus.

Some of the factors that minimize the risk of cancer, such as a healthy diet, eliminating smoking, or avoiding exposure to harmful chemicals and X-rays, are within our power to control. Others, such as age, gender, race, genetic history, or environmental hazards, are not. Direct causes for cancer remain elusive, except in the case of lung cancer, which has been directly linked to a history of smoking. The risk of developing lung cancer drops appreciably when one stops smoking. Risk factors for other types of cancer such as breast cancer are less predictable. Early detection in the form of physical exams, breast self-exams, mammograms, or biopsy are especially important. The American Geriatrics Society recommends mammograms every two to three years for women sixty-five to eighty-five years old. With some cancers, early detection offers the possibility of cure or substantial remission with years of symptom-free life.

Many factors influence the treatment plan for cancer patients. Age and stage of disease are two of these. Despite the advances in breast cancer treatment, controversy remains regarding the best type of therapy. Possible methods of treatment include surgery, chemotherapy, radiotherapy, endocrine therapy, or some combination of these methods. In older women, the issue of comorbidity (evidence of associated diseases such as heart disease, hypertension, or diabetes) appears to be an influential factor in selecting cancer treatment.

The question of surviving an acute or chronic illness such as cancer is an especially important one for older women. There are predictable emotional and social consequences, often experienced as anxiety or depression. The task of healthy living in spite of an uncertain medical future is challenging. In addition to competent medical care, coping skills, support systems, and a sense of hope and purpose are critical. Support groups such as those sponsored by the American Cancer Society can be particularly helpful to cancer survivors. Hospice care can also provide an option when the expected outcome is not cure or survival.

Osteoporosis

Osteoporosis, a metabolic bone disorder, affects some 25 million people, 80 percent of them older women. Each year 1.5 million fractures, primarily of the vertebra, hip, and wrist, can be attributed to osteoporosis. The National Osteoporosis Foundation reports that the loss in quality of life for people over sixty-five who suffer a severe fracture is staggering. Many of the 300,000 women a year who fracture a hip do not return to full activity. At least half need help with daily living activities, 15 to 20 percent end up in long-term care institutions, and 12 to 20 percent die from complications after a fracture.

Women lose bone mass as they age. At age fifty, a woman has a 50 percent chance of suffering from an osteoporosis-related fracture sometime in her remaining years. By the time a woman reaches eighty, she will have lost approximately 47 percent of her trabecular (interior meshwork) of bone. This debilitating disease and its physical pain causes great psychological and social problems for older women.

Osteoporosis is also known as the silent disease, since diagnosis often comes only after a person sustains a fracture. Screening and diagnosis can be difficult since low bone-density alone does not necessarily indicate osteoporosis. Diagnostic tests to measure bone mass are not routinely done and are not always covered by health insurance plans. Results of these tests also vary with respect to the site measured and the precision, accuracy, and dose of radiation. However, a woman affected by the following risk factors may benefit from a bone-density assessment as part of a medical exam: age, sex, body build, family history, and race are the commonly cited nonmodifiable risk factors. Risk factors that can be modified include: loss of estrogen, calcium deficiency, sedentary lifestyle, smoking, excessive alcohol and caffeine consumption, and the use of certain medications such as steroids and diuretics.

Although there is no cure for osteoporosis, it is to some extent preventable and treatable. Three common approaches are hormone replacement therapies, nutrition interventions such as calcium additives, and exercise programs. These strategies are aimed at maintaining or stabilizing bone mass and preventing further loss. For women who are not candidates for estrogen replacement therapy, synthetic salmon calcitronin may be an option. Experts differ in their opinions regarding the use and value of these treatments. Many women have learned to cope with osteoporosis by getting advice on how to manage pain, adjust their diets, exercise properly, adapt their lifestyle, and cultivate social and psychological support. Other sources of information are listed at the back of this book.

Diabetes

Diabetes is very common in the elderly—40 percent of those over sixty-five are diabetic, and women are at especially high risk for developing this disease. It is not only dangerous in and of itself, but people with diabetes often develop complications such as kidney failure and blindness, resulting in severe disability and even death. Diabetes is a syndrome with at least four different types. The two main types, Type I and Type II, differ in cause and treatment. Diabetes is believed to be due to a lack of availability of insulin, which aids in the metabolism of carbohydrates, proteins, and fats that maintain the body's energy balance. Obesity is the most obvious risk factor, but hypertension, smoking, and chronic alcohol intake also affect diabetes. Other risks are high cholesterol, inactivity, and high stress.

The warning signs for both major types of diabetes include fatigue, thirst, frequent urination, slow healing of cuts and bruises, urinary tract and vaginal infection and itching, steady weight gain or sudden weight loss, dental disease, and difficulty with eyesight. In Type II, these come on gradually and may be mistaken for normal aging.

Older women with diabetes need a comprehensive treatment plan that includes medication, medical monitoring, diet, exercise, and stress reduction. Diabetes is an example of the value of self-care, in terms of both prevention and health maintenance. People who have diabetes should always carry medical identification.

Arthritis

Arthritis is the leading cause of disability for older women. By age sixty-five to seventy, about 80 percent of all women have arthritic symptoms. Arthritis is a group of diseases characterized by stiffness, chronic pain, and loss of movement. There are over a hundred different types of arthritis, each with its own symptoms. Little is known about what causes most types. Some seem to run in families; others seem to be related to imbalances in body chemistry or immune system problems. Two common types are osteoarthritis, a degenerative joint disease, and rheumatoid arthritis, a systemic connective tissue disorder. Rheumatism is an older word for these symptoms.

It may not be possible to prevent or cure arthritis, but its symptoms can, in most cases, be alleviated, joint function can be improved, and disability can be prevented or reduced. Symptoms of pain and stiffness may arise from a variety of causes, and careful diagnosis can determine what treatment is appropriate. Treatment is generally a combination of joint protection, exercise, medication, heat and cold treatments, and weight control. Control of inflammation and pain is also essential for managing rheumatic disorders, and a variety of prescription and nonprescription drugs are available to do this. Only 3 percent of those with the disease are seriously disabled.

Older women with arthritis can learn to adapt to its impact on their lives by learning new strategies for managing pain, combating feelings of helplessness, and modifying daily activities to compensate for reduced mobility. Home health care, home-delivered meals, and homemaker or chore services are particularly helpful when basic self-care or household tasks are difficult to accomplish.

Alzheimer's Disease

Alzheimer's disease is one of a group of late-life dementias that are caused by diseases of the brain. Senility (a loss of mental faculties associated with old age) was an earlier, catchall term that was often used to describe these symptoms, but it no longer has real meaning. Late-life dementia is a neurological disorder that has no relationship with a person's previous intelligence, education, or mental health. Because these disorders are devastating to a person's basic behavioral, psychological, and social functioning, they represent some of the most feared risks of aging.

Alzheimer's disease now accounts for an estimated two-thirds of all dementias in the U.S. and it is the term now most frequently used for late-life dementia. It afflicts an estimated 5 percent of those over sixty-five, rising to 25 to 50 percent of those over eighty-five. This disease and related dementias affect women, for four reasons: first, women live longer than men, thus increasing the risk of dementia in later life; second, more women than men develop the disease; third, women traditionally have assumed the caregiver role, women are more likely than men to provide care for spouses, parents, and parents-in-law who have dementia; and fourth, more women than men provide direct nursing care to patients with dementia in nursing homes and hospitals.

Researchers have developed many theories concerning the causes of Alzheimer's disease in the past decade, but none that explain its onset. There is currently no treatment that cures, halts the progress of, or has a predictable and reliable effect on Alzheimer's disease. Some symptoms, such as uncontrollable agitation, sleeplessness, night wandering, memory loss, and confusion, may be reduced by drugs or environmental adaptations. However, all drugs, especially those that alter mental function, can have negative effects and should be monitored by a physician. The use of multiple drugs, especially a combination of over-the-counter drugs and alcohol, can result in drug toxicity, which may increase rather than reduce symptoms.

Coping with dementia requires medical and behavioral interventions to manage disruptive symptoms, knowledge to optimize environmental conditions, and caregiver support to avoid burnout. The local and national chapters of the Alzheimer's Disease and Related Disorders Association offer hot lines, support groups, and newsletters to benefit those living with dementia.

RISK FACTORS TO AGING WELL

It is well-known that the six diseases reviewed above are major threats to our health and life. We worry about them, we fear them, and our lives will be changed by their impact on us and those we love. But how well we age is also likely to be affected by a cluster of risk factors not directly related to the onset of a life-threatening disease such as cancer or heart disease. Reducing these risk factors often prevents more serious illness and disability.

In 1990, "The Second Fifty Years" report, issued by a committee at the Institute of Medicine of the National Academy of Science, identified thirteen risk factors and causes of disability in older people: misuse of medications, social isolation, physical inactivity, falls, sensory loss, depression, dental problems, lack of screening for cancer, malnutrition, smoking, high blood-pressure, osteoporosis, and infectious diseases.

This report urged health professionals to go beyond medicine's two traditional goals—to cure and prevent disease—to the new goal of preserving and improving the quality of life for older people. By emphasizing risk factors that affect large numbers of older people and are to some extent within our control, the report urged us to take care of our own health. Even though we can't live a risk-free life, we can improve the quality of our life in the face of predictable health problems, such as loss of physical functions, lifestyle health risks, and threats to our psychosocial health.

Loss of Physical Functions

Perhaps the most devastating threats to unencumbered aging, and those we fear the most, are losses of physical functions.

Sensory Loss and Falls

Whether due to processes of aging, underlying disease, or a combination of both, the partial or full loss of any sensory function has significant implications for the older woman. Her independence and her quality of life may be markedly reduced by severe or multiple sensory losses of vision, hearing, taste, and perception. Even though these changes may be viewed as an inevitable and minor aggravation of old age, they can still dramatically affect us. Periodic testing for hearing loss or visual impairment is important. Early detection of cataracts, glaucoma, macular degeneration, or diabetic retinopathy can prevent later disability.

Only a small percentage of older people are blind, but loss of vision dramatically increases the likelihood of falls, the most common cause of fatal injury in older persons. Injury from falls has been cited as the leading cause of accidental death among people over seventy-five. The most common cause of falls is tripping or stumbling over something at home, often related to poor coordination or poor eyesight. Strategies for making one's home safer in order to prevent falls and accidents are discussed in chapter four. Many falls also occur as a result of dizziness, a side effect of chronic illnesses such as high blood-pressure and the medications used to treat them.

Hearing loss can also have a major impact on everyday life. Despite the availability of hearing aids, a woman may postpone or resist using one because she feels self-conscious, confused, or angry about her loss of hearing. Loss of vision or hearing can make every social encounter stressful and tiring, leading to a withdrawal from social contact and an increasing sense of isolation and dependence.

An older woman faced with a significant sensory loss needs help in learning to adapt to impairment in order to maintain her sense of personal control. Adaptive devices such as large-print books, audiotapes, transportation assistance, homemaking agencies, or delivery services can help her maintain her independence.

Urinary Incontinence
In addition to these sensory losses, another chronic condition that can dramatically affect our everyday life is urinary incontinence. More than ten million adults, three-quarters of whom are women, have bladder control problems. Half of all women experience temporary urinary incontinence at some point in their lives and about one-third develop a regular problem. After age sixty, incontinence is twice as common among women than men. It is a major factor in nursing home admissions, and more than half of all nursing home residents are incontinent. Most of those who suffer with urinary incontinence can be cured or significantly improved, yet only about half ever seek help from a health professional. Incontinence can often be prevented or improved by simple exercises to strengthen the muscles that support the bladder. Other treatments include drugs or surgery.

Lifestyle Health Problems
Various aspects of our lifestyle significantly affect our health. With some help, many of these issues are manageable.

Misuse of Medications and Drugs
Older Americans use 4.5 million drug prescriptions (30 percent of all those prescribed) and 3.5 million over-the-counter drugs annually. It is estimated that 10 to 15 percent of the older population, or more

than 2.5 million people, are dependent on alcohol, prescription drugs, or over-the-counter medicines. Even though medications can improve health and cure illness, they can also cause serious and life-threatening problems if overused or misused. *Polypharmacy* is the term used to describe taking too many, or excessive amounts of, drugs at a time. But improper use of medications also involves taking less than is prescribed or stopping too soon. This is common among older women, who may be given prescriptions by several physicians for different conditions. Approximately 62 percent of all visits to physicians involve prescriptions for one or more drugs. Older women are also more likely than men to receive psychotropic (such as antianxiety or antidepressant) prescriptions, probably because they have relatively high rates of diagnosis for depression, anxiety, and psychoneurotic complaints for which tranquilizers and sedatives are often prescribed.

The National Council on Patient Information and Education recommends that women know each medicine's name, what it is supposed to do, how much to take, when to take it, how long to continue taking it, and whether to expect side effects or adverse reactions and what to do if they occur, especially when they are taken in combination with other drugs. In addition, you should know whether any foods or beverages should be avoided, and whether any activities such as driving a car should be avoided. Pharmacists should furnish this information when dispensing prescriptions. Ask for it!

Another factor that contributes to the misuse of medications and drugs is the overuse of alcohol. Alcohol used in combination with other drugs can cause serious harmful reactions for older women. Consistent overuse of alcohol (more than one to two ounces per day) can increase the risk of liver disease, neurological problems, falls, and other accidents. Some warning signs of alcoholism are short-term memory loss, slurred speech, depression, social isolation, neglected appearance, and malnutrition. These symptoms are often misinterpreted as signs of aging or dementia. Older women are often ashamed of their alcohol addiction, but help is available at most hospitals, or from organizations such as Women for Sobriety (1-800-333-1606), the National Council on Alcoholism and Drug Dependence (1-800-622-2255), or Alcoholics Anonymous (listed in your telephone book).

Malnutrition

There is ample evidence that dietary excesses or deficiencies can lead to disease conditions and affect their treatment and recovery. The *New York Times* recently reported that as many as 50 percent of women over the age of sixty-five are malnourished because they consume too few calories, proteins, and essential vitamins and minerals for good health. Extreme thinness is linked to susceptibility to certain diseases, including lung diseases, fatal infection, ulcers, and anemia. According to recent research at the NIH Obesity Research Center at St. Luke's-Roosevelt Hospital in New York, being thinner than normal can be dangerous for elderly people. Obesity, the opposite of thinness, is also associated with health problems, such as hypertension, stroke, heart disease, high cholesterol, diabetes mellitus, and osteoarthritis. Many elderly women believe they are overweight when they are not. As we grow older, some lean muscle tissue is replaced with fatty tissue that can cause weight gain. Even if we stay the same weight, we will have more fat proportionately at eighty than we did at forty. Using diet pills and special diet products, as well as following diets promising spectacular weight loss, are a poor solution to an underlying problem of poor nutrition.

Older women are particularly vulnerable to malnutrition, for a number of reasons. Money is often limited. Diseases accompanying aging affect nutritional needs and metabolism. Eating habits and diet are also greatly affected by decreasing mobility. Even getting to the grocery store or opening a can or bottle can be a major obstacle. Living alone also decreases the desire to prepare and eat a healthy balanced diet. Arranging for a service such as Meals on Wheels, attending a senior center, arranging transportation to the grocery store, or inviting a friend to meals can help.

Smoking

Smoking takes a toll on our bodies. Twenty percent of older adults are currently smokers, and respiratory infections are the fourth leading cause of death in those over sixty-five. The risk of lung cancer—the number one cancer killer of women—increases with age. Smoking is also associated with lower food intake and other damaging health behaviors. Even though the risks from smoking increase with age and with the number of years one has smoked, it is never too late to give up smoking and reduce the damage smoking can do. Quitting at any age causes the mortality rate to drop. It is reassuring to know that a high percentage of those who try to quit do succeed. Many quit on their own. For others, mutual-help groups and cessation programs work well. The rewards for success are better health, a longer life, and the pride of being in control of one's body.

Physical Inactivity

There is increasing evidence that physical activity (such as walking, hiking, or swimming) is a key component of healthy aging and not only safeguards health, but improves it. A Duke University Center for the Study of Aging report suggested that inactivity causes depression, poor circulation, weak muscles, stiff joints, shortness of breath, loss of bone mass, and fatigue. While daily activities keep us moving, they are usually not sufficient to promote and maintain fitness. A movement program, often offered free or at low cost at a senior center, can increase flexibility, cardiovascular endurance, and muscular strength. Even though our physical strength or movement may be restricted, we can still benefit from moderate and regular exercise.

Dental Health Problems

Though aging itself does not necessarily lead to tooth loss, decay, or disease, proper dental care is just as important for older people as it is for the young. Nevertheless, more than half of all people over sixty-five have not been to a dentist in at least five years or have never been to one. The risk of losing teeth, developing cavities, or periodontal disease increases as we age, and women have higher rates of tooth loss than men. Although many people believe that tooth loss is a natural part of aging, this is not the case. Tooth loss can prevent us from eating well, and dental problems can lead to a whole range of potentially debilitating and isolating conditions among older people. Daily brushing and regular visits to a dentist for cleaning and checkups are good insurance for dental health.

Threats to Our Psychosocial Health

Most persons cope with changes in their lives as they grow older relatively well. At the same time, our desire to feel well, strong, and in control of our health creates legitimate anxiety and stress. Wisdom tells us, and research confirms, that there is a basic link between one's sense of control over life, the psychological supports of that control (self-esteem, confidence, autonomy, and power over choices), and the immune system's resistance to disease or decline. Gene Cohen, director of the Washington, D.C., Center on Aging reports that the relationship between health and mental health is strongest in later life, and that in the face of chronic depression or stress, biological changes occur that have a negative effect on the immune system and render people more vulnerable to disease.

Betty Friedan, in her book *The Fountain of Age*, also cites research suggesting that factors such as isolation, lack of intimate companions, decrease of purposeful activity, malnutrition, or physical inactivity account for a larger share of the decline in the immune systems of elders than is generally recognized.

Social Isolation

Research shows that those who maintain strong bonds with family, friends, or neighbors actually have lower death and illness rates. Because so many older women become full-time caregivers or find themselves single and living alone, isolation from other people is common. Maintaining social contacts also becomes increasingly difficult when physical frailty is a problem. However, loneliness has been found to result more from lack of emotional closeness than the number of contacts people have.

Depression

As we grow older we become particularly vulnerable to changes in our social situations. Depression in later life is often a response to losses, either physical, social, or financial. It is also a side effect of some medications. Deaths of loved ones, relocation to an unfamiliar place, unplanned retirement, or increased social isolation can bring about emotional changes that trigger forgetfulness, confusion, disorientation, and depression. Symptoms of depression include a despondent mood, loss of interest in usual activities, loss of appetite, sleeplessness, feelings of worthlessness or hopelessness, guilt, self-reproach, or suicidal thoughts or behavior.

Depression often seems naturally connected to specific events, but the emotional pain and sadness following personal losses should lessen over time. Sadness that is pervasive becomes a disorder when it interferes with someone's usual state of functioning for an extended period of time (for example, more than six months following a loved one's death). Correct diagnosis is extremely important, since the mental symptoms of depression often resemble those of Alzheimer's disease and can be misdiagnosed as Alzheimer's or as senility and left untreated. Many people with clinical depression can be successfully treated with a combination of medication and group therapy, classes, or workshops designed to develop positive feelings and increased self-esteem. The first step in getting help for depression is to recognize the symptoms and not blame yourself for feeling depressed. The next is to ask for help from a senior center, mental health professional, or medical practitioner.

BUILDING AND MAINTAINING HEALTH

Earlier in this chapter, the importance of building and maintaining physical, social, and psychological fitness was stressed as a goal for aging well. This goal implies action on our part rather than passivity. There are no magic wands or potions for ensuring good health, no fountains of youth, no products that cure all ills, no vitamins that prevent all ailments. However, growing old well—maintaining and even improving our physical and emotional health—is something over which we have more control than ever before. George Solomon, one of the founders of the new study of psychoeuroimmunology (how the mind, stress, and the immune system interact), studied physically healthy older people from sixty-seven to ninety-seven. All of them were functioning well, with no life-threatening illness. He found them to have a high incidence of "hardiness," which involves control, commitment, and challenge.

Many illnesses and disabilities in later life are chronic problems related to lifestyle and health habits. Sometimes we can do something to avoid these illnesses, and sometimes we have to learn to live with them. We can't turn back the clock, but we might keep the hands from moving faster than they might. Scientific research is showing that our health choices—positive or negative—greatly affect how we age. What we do every day to care for our bodies, our minds, and our spirits does matter. If caring for ourselves and committing to being as healthy as possible are related to healthy aging, we need to ask, what is my blueprint for action? Our answers deserve careful thought and attention. The following four steps will guide you.

Begin at the Beginning

Take an inventory of your current health status. The risk factors discussed earlier in this chapter are a good place to start. How well do you practice everyday habits of good health? How do you rate in the proper use of medications, social and physical activity, good nutrition, avoidance of smoking? A professional medical assessment is essential to complete this picture. A medical problem may be a symptom of disease, rather than a normal part of aging, and we should seek solutions for it. Finding affordable health care is discussed later in this chapter.

Competent medical assessment also involves having a physician you trust: one who knows you and your medical history and can add to your sense of security about receiving effective medical treatment. Finding a good physician is essential to your health and peace of mind. A thorough assessment, if ordered by your physician, may be at least partly covered by Medicare.

As patients, we need to learn to be assertive, polite, and persistent with professionals who make decisions about our life. Our rights as patients include the right of informed consent, which means that before you permit anyone in a medical or mental health setting to do anything to you, they must first inform you fully as to what is planned; the risks and potential benefits of the treatment plan, and alternative forms of treatment, including the option of no treatment at all.

When you meet with your physician:

+ Write down in advance all your symptoms and the questions you want to ask.

+ Write down or bring with you all the medications you take, including over-the-counter remedies and vitamin supplements.

+ Bring someone along with you to your appointment.

+ Listen carefully to the diagnosis, treatment options and their consequences, recommendations for treatment, prognosis, and cost of treatment.

* Don't make any immediate decisions about your treatment if you feel unsure or uncomfortable about the choices.

* Consider a second opinion if you are uncertain.

Create a Plan

Any plan for changing what we are currently doing about the state of our health involves taking a more active role in staying well, or helping our bodies heal or adjust to disabilities or health problems. What we do every day does matter.

Deciding to get medical advice or a medical examination can be an important step toward better health. Making lifestyle changes in diet, exercise, smoking, managing stress, improving safety measures in our home, or taking medications with care may be equally vital. Contacting a resource agency or friend to expand your personal network of activities may also be at the top of your agenda.

Making a plan to care for yourself starts with choosing one or two aspects of your lifestyle you sincerely want to change, then deciding why, how, and when you will make those changes. Perhaps the most important part of your plan is convincing yourself that it is absolutely vital that you alter this practice now, not tomorrow or next year.

Build Success in Small Steps

Whether your plan includes actions designed to nurture your body, mind, or spirit, it will increase your sense of power over your life. Habits are like the bone structure of our lives—the firm structure upon which we can rely, the routines we follow but don't think about very much. Some of our habits have worked well for us throughout our lives, but now need to be changed. It is not true that as aging progresses we become less flexible, less able to change. Change and renewal are possible at any age.

Change begins with an intention, inspiration, or decision. Inspiration can come from new information, by physical changes, by the advice of someone we care for and respect, or simply because we are confronted by the awareness that we have limited time left to take care of ourselves.

Focus on one or two actions at a time to avoid overwhelming yourself. For example, a decision to improve your diet, get more exercise, stop smoking, join a group at a community center, get a medical checkup, and take your medication more consistently is probably too ambitious to be successful.

Change happens when you know what works for you. A clean-slate approach may be your style of change, but small manageable steps may be more promising. Many habits interact. Changing one habit may help you change others. For example, if you are trying to walk more often and drink fruit juice or herbal tea instead of coffee, invite a neighbor to join you for your walk and some tea, and make it a social occasion.

Reward, Evaluate, and Renew Your Efforts

Reward yourself! No matter which approach to change you choose, watch out for procrastination. Failure to make progress one day simply means the next day is a new opportunity. Remember, resistance is a normal and predictable part of change. It is not something to avoid, but something to recognize. When you feel stuck, call a friend, create a new strategy, ask for help from others, or read something inspiring.

Keep a record or journal as a progress report. Note obstacles and triumphs and remember to reward yourself for each success. A special lunch, listening to your favorite music, or just feeling proud of yourself are simple but symbolic rewards that will pay dividends in increased energy and satisfaction, additional aspects of good health.

The Economics of Health Care

We want the best medical care available, but as older women we face a variety of problems in paying the cost. Medical care costs continue to rise and consume an increasing percentage of our income. In 1994, older Americans spent 23 percent of their income on health care expenses. We also face a patchwork of poorly coordinated agencies, services, and programs in different locations with different eligibility rules and policies. Some of us mistakenly assume Medicare will cover all the costs of our medical care after we reach our sixty-fifth birthday. Medicare does cover most acute conditions in a hospital, however, most older people also need preventive care, care of chronic conditions on an outpatient basis, or supportive care. The AARP's Public Policy Institute recently reported that nearly half of older Americans have no coverage for prescribed medicines.

Getting Health Care

There are two distinct types of medical care that you or your caretakers may have to deal with: acute care and long-term care. Acute care refers to the costs associated with treatment for illness or injury in hospitals or by doctors on an outpatient basis. Hospital bills and most doctor bills incurred in a hospital are paid for by one, or a combination of the following: Medicare, private Medicare supplement insurance (Medigap), other private insurance, or a health maintenance organization (HMO).

Long-term care refers to personal care needed by people with a mental or physical chronic, degenerative illness or disability who require continued assistance with daily activities. This care may be provided at home, in community-based facilities such as an adult day-care center, or in a nursing home. The cost is rarely covered by acute care medical insurance or Medicare. Aside from the patient paying directly for long-term care, Medicaid or long-term care insurance may cover some or all of the cost.

Paying for Health Care

Major sources of funding for the health care of older people are public programs such as Medicare and Medicaid, or private insurance companies and health maintenance organizations. (Additional information on how these programs affect nursing home coverage and long-term care can be found in chapters six and seven.) Brief descriptions follow:

Medicare is the federal health insurance program for people age sixty-five or older (and some disabled people under age sixty-five). To find out if you qualify for Medicare call your local Social Security office before your sixty-fifth birthday, or at the time you become disabled. You must apply for Medicare; it is not an automatic benefit. Medicare is divided into two parts. Both have deductible requirements and coverage limitations.

Part A Medicare coverage pays for most in-patient hospital care. Patients must pay a $760 deductible per hospital benefit period in 1997. Some skilled nursing home care (up to 100 days of coverage) with variable deductible amounts is provided. Some home health care and hospice services are also covered. For those who meet Social Security or Railroad Retirement qualifications, there is no monthly charge for this coverage. Others who are eligible may purchase coverage for $188 to $289 per month (1996 cost), depending on the number of earned quarters of Social Security credit.

Part B Medicare coverage is optional. It pays for doctors' services, outpatient care, outpatient physical and speech therapy, ambulance services, some medical equipment and supplies, and other services. There is a yearly deductible amount and a 20 percent copayment for services if your physician accepts assignment (if not, the copayment could be larger). The monthly premium of $43.80 (in 1997) is automatically deducted from an individual's Social Security check if this coverage is selected. Even if an individual is not covered by Social Security, she may choose to purchase Part B and be billed for it.

Medicare is not a comprehensive health care program. It pays only for what is medically necessary, which, for many, is less than half of many health care costs. Most older women want to supplement Medicare with a Medicare supplement insurance policy usually referred to as a Medigap policy, unless they join an HMO. In that case, a supplemental insurance policy is not necessary.

Medicare Supplemental Insurance (Medigap) policies are insurance plans sold by private insurance companies which cover part or all of Medicare's copayments and deductibles. Some offer other benefits not covered by Medicare, such as prescription drugs. Medigap policies differ widely, with premiums from $45 to $200 a month. It is important to compare benefits and costs before purchasing. Information and help in comparing policies is available from local health insurance counseling offices. A toll-free number to locate these offices is listed in the resource section of this book. A Guide to Health Insurance for People with Medicare can also be requested from the Department of Health and Human Services.

Health Maintenance Organizations (HMOs) provide comprehensive health care, including hospitalization and outpatient care, with small or no premiums for enrollees with Medicare coverage. A small copayment is often required for medical services. Some HMOs provide additional benefits not covered by Medicare, such as preventive care, prescription drugs, hearing, and eye exams. HMO enrollees are usually locked into using only physicians, health professionals, and facilities contracted by the HMO, except for emergency care and out-of-area urgent care. A Medigap insurance policy is not needed.

Retirement and Employer Plans may include health insurance as a retirement benefit. If you are older than age sixty-five but still employed, you can choose to be covered under your employer's health plan, along with Medicare coverage.

Medicaid is a state and federally funded program providing health insurance coverage to low-income people who meet specific eligibility requirements. Medicaid programs vary greatly from state to state regarding eligibility, benefits, and payment for services. Eligibility can be determined through local county Social Service departments or Legal Assistance for Seniors.

The *Qualified Medicare Beneficiary Program* assists people whose assets aren't low enough to qualify for Medicaid by paying for Medicare premiums.

The *Specified Low-Income Medicare Beneficiary Program,* also administered by the Social Service Administration, assists low-income people by paying their Medicare premiums.

GETTING ON WITH LIVING WELL

The purpose of this chapter has been to briefly explore what is known about healthy living among older women, with particular attention to preventing and overcoming illness and impairment. Sometimes this means recognizing the changes that come with aging and doing what we can about them. This may simply mean getting more information, a cane to assist with walking, or a hearing aid for better communication. It may also mean undergoing medical treatment or surgery, changing one's lifestyle, and, most importantly, developing a positive attitude, so that "in spite of it all," we can get on with living. The desire and determination to age well empowers us to make decisions and choices about our own health.

Chapter Three

FINANCIAL LITERACY:
The Economics of Aging

*It's time for women to take the next step—to make financial literacy
the rule rather than the exception.*
—from Investing Your Way

MONEY, OR THE LACK of it, affects us throughout our lives, but
when we're over sixty it plays an even greater role in how and where
we live, and in a whole spectrum of options and choices about our
daily lives. At a deeper personal level, our financial resources affect
our self-esteem, relationships with our families, and even our sense of
overall satisfaction with the way we have lived our lives. Few of us
can live without worrying, or at least thinking seriously, about money.
Even when a long, stable marriage or work record has fostered
assumptions about our financial security, divorce, widowhood, the
disability of a partner or oneself, or simply living longer than we
expected can seriously threaten those cherished assumptions.

FINANCIAL FACTS OF LIFE FOR OLDER WOMEN

We hear endless debates about the economic facts of aging. Statistics
describe us as either rich, selfish greedy geezers or poor, helpless vic-

tims. But as in most statistically based arguments, there is some fact as well as fiction in every number. Overall, today's elders have higher living standards than any sixty-five-plus generation in U.S. history. However, there is still considerable poverty among older women, and huge numbers of us are living barely above poverty level, with social security as our major financial resource.

This big picture makes it clear that the world of money is different for men and women. In her informative and practical book, *Money and the Mature Woman,* Frances Leonard emphasizes these differences: Women start retirement with less money than men; women live longer than men; and most women die single, while most men die married. Women of our generation have also grown up with contradictory and often disabling beliefs about money. The importance of these differences and their impact on our lives is profound. Although our personal attitudes and skills partially explain these facts, explanations for these differences also come from our place in history and in our culture.

Women Start Retirement with Less Money Than Men

Although today's older women have benefited from increased opportunities to earn money, our participation in the paid workforce has not often translated to a more secure financial life after sixty. Women's retirement income is only 58 percent of men's, and older women are 75 percent more likely to be impoverished than elderly males. The U.S. Census Bureau's 1996 Current Population Report stated that the median income of women sixty-five and older was $8,189 (compared to $14,548 for men). Older people living alone (divorced, widowed, or unmarried) were poorer than married couples, and the highest poverty rates were associated with African-American and Hispanic women living alone.

The numbers describing the overall economic status of older women paint a bleak picture. Not surprisingly, the poorest group strongly relies on Social Security, while the wealthiest depends large-ly on income from assets and investments.

Even though most women have worked for pay at some time, they often have been employed in low-paying, part-time, or temporary work with the reduced likelihood of accumulating pensions and Social Security credit. Only one out of five women sixty-five and older receive any type of company pension, and the average Social Security benefit for retired women workers in 1993 was less than minimum wage. There are many reasons for this; but it's due mostly to the spo-radic nature of women's participation in the workforce. Women often put careers on hold to raise families or to respond to the demands of others whose needs are deemed to take priority.

Almost every older woman has spent part of her life in the eco-nomic vacuum of women who don't work. Work for no pay includes taking care of a husband, child, or aging relative at home, or provid-ing volunteer services in the community. This is work that would have monetary value in the paid job market, but not when it is performed by a woman at home. Women have provided as much as $18 billion in volunteer hours in one year. This figure applies only to volunteer work done outside the home, not to housework, caregiving, or myriad other duties performed by most women at home. A woman doing this "women's work" accrues no benefits such as disability insurance, unemployment compensation, pension plans, or health coverage. If she is married, her financial security is thus tied to her husband's earnings and benefits.

Women Live Longer Than Men

Another major factor affecting the financial security of older women is the fact that our money will probably need to last longer to provide for the extra post-wage years we can expect to live. According to the AARP, women reaching age sixty-five in 1990 could expect to live an additional nineteen years (15.3 years for men). Most retirement income sources such as pensions and investment income are not adjusted to keep pace with inflation or fluctuating interest rates. We are also vulnerable to increasing out-of-pocket expenses for health and long-term care. Women live longer but often die poorer than they expected.

Most Women Die Single; Most Men Die Married

Women outlive men and have usually married older men. It is not surprising, therefore, that 85 percent of women die single and 85 percent of men die married. Since marital status is the single most reliable predictor of wealth at all ages, single older women are at the greatest risk of poverty. In 1992, the most recent U.S. Census data shows that more than 27 percent of single older women were poor, and another 14 percent were near-poor. Even though some expenses may decrease after the death of a partner, it is estimated that the cost of maintaining a one-person household is at least 80 percent of the cost of maintaining a two-person household.

The price of singlehood often first confronts a woman when divorce shifts her financial status from being tied to her husband's earnings and benefits to being on her own financially. A divorce settlement should always consider the husband's pension as an important asset. A recent study shows that following a midlife divorce, a woman's income usually drops dramatically.

Economics Anxiety Shapes Our Attitudes

In addition to these economic facts of life, many of us have grown up in a time when our attitudes about money have been repeatedly challenged. Messages from our youth included: *Men know more than I do. Someone will take care of me. It's not nice to talk about money. I shouldn't have to think about it. Tomorrow will take care of itself. I just can't learn about money, it's too difficult.* These attitudes may have served us adequately as long as we assumed that dependence on a strong, caring, stable husband/provider would make our dreams of security come true. But for many of us, singlehood, divorce, widowhood, or remarriage and other life changes have challenged us to become more financially independent and competent.

It's not surprising that math and economics anxiety, as well as outmoded beliefs about money, have made an impression on our view of a woman's place in the world. But these assumptions can have devastating results in our later years. Even though long-term financial planning has often been the responsibility of the men in our lives, we need now more than ever to manage our money and financial resources effectively. Keeping household financial records, paying bills, and balancing a checkbook are basic skills necessary to maintain financial health and security. But there is much more we can learn to increase our financial competence, not only for the sake of personal pride, but to increase the options and control we have over how we live. The absence of money decreases our choices in all areas of our life: health, housing, activities, and the support services we can afford.

BUILDING FINANCIAL COMPETENCE

There are no magic formulas or shortcuts to financial health for an older woman. We are extremely diverse in our knowledge and experience with finances. But no matter what our circumstances, it is never too late to take stock of what we have, become more aware of how we are currently using and managing our financial resources, plan for changes, and find information and assistance to help carry out our plans.

One thing is certain: During this stage of life, our financial needs and personal circumstances will probably change. Unexpected sources of income may be found, such as inheritance, or reduced income and increased expenses may force us to make changes.

Six questions and their answers will build your financial competence. The first three determine the facts about what you own, what you owe, where your income comes from, and where it goes. The next three offer guidance for managing and planning for the future, and finding help and advice.

What Is Your Financial Net Worth?

Before you can make wise decisions as a financially competent person, you need to know the facts about what you own and what you owe. The first essential step is to determine your net worth (the sum of the value of all your assets minus the sum of all your liabilities). Whether you own nothing of major value or a great deal, this step is necessary. Once you have determined your net worth, you have a picture of your current financial status. The Personal Assets Worksheet and the Net Worth Worksheet at the end of this chapter will help you clarify your economic situation.

Assets are anything you own that has value. Assets include cash, checking and savings accounts, investments, money owed to you, life insurance with cash value, retirement funds, social security benefits and pensions, real estate, and personal property such as automobiles, furniture, and collectibles.

In addition to the current value of your own assets, you need to know (if you are married) what you and/or your husband legally own. The principal methods of co-ownership of property are tenancy in common and joint tenancy. Other ways to legally own property, such as tenancy by the entirety, are available only under certain circumstances and are not discussed here. Who is listed as owner or co-owner of each property? This information is especially important in second marriages, where ownership of assets may have specific implications for taxes and inheritance.

Tenancy in common allows property to be owned in equal or unequal shares. Each owner's share can be bequeathed to that owner's heirs, and not necessarily to the other cotenants.

Joint tenancy with right of survivorship provides for two or more people to own property together. When one person dies, all that person's share goes to the other person(s). The property can be real estate, securities, or bank accounts. This provision cannot be changed by a will, and property in such an account is not probated.

Liabilities are claims against your assets. They include mortgages, loans, and outstanding debts. Again, consider the type of ownership and name(s) of owner or co-owner. Your husband's liabilities should also be included.

What Is Your Annual Income and How Do You Spend It?

The next step in assessing your financial picture is to determine what your income is, where it comes from, and how it is being spent. Look first at checkbook stubs and credit card statements to find where your money has gone. Figures for January through December for the past year are most useful and convenient for this because tax returns coincide with these dates. Complete the Annual Income and Expenses Worksheet at the end of this chapter to determine your money patterns.

Income includes all sources (record the annual amount received). If you are married, distribute the income into the Self and Spouse columns to show who earns it or who owns the assets that produce it. It's best to list gross income, or the total amount you receive before deductions. This way you can include taxes and other deductions as part of your expenses and keep track of them.

Expenses include everything you spent during the year. Again, if you are married, use the Self and Spouse columns to separate personal expenses such as clothing, automobiles, and gifts, to get a clear picture of your spending. Include investments, savings, taxes, and so on. Total expenses, of course, should equal total income.

If your miscellaneous spending category is larger than 10 percent of your income, start keeping track of how you spend your money! Listing cash expenditures in a small notebook at the end of each day is one way to inform yourself about where your money goes. If you cannot account for all your spending, adjust the miscellaneous category until income and expenses are the same. If expenses exceed total income, find out why.

Where Does Your Income Come From?

The three traditional sources of retirement income are Social Security, pensions, and investments or savings. Income from Social Security and pensions is fixed by past work and marital history. Investments or savings, the third major source of retirement income, may be limited and subject to fluctuations in interest rates. Other potential sources of income, such as employment or home equity, may need to be explored in order to stretch finances to cover expenses. However, inheritance (marriage or family), insurance benefits, or community and government programs may also provide additional income.

Because our financial resources are so important in determining how and where we live in our later years, this section summarizes major facts about Social Security, Supplemental Security Income, pensions, savings and financial investments, insurance, employment, and home equity.

Social Security

Most people over sixty-five rely on Social Security as a major source of income. In fact, one in four women age sixty-five or older relies on Social Security for at least 90 percent of her income. Social Security benefits are due to everyone who meets eligibility requirements. Benefits are determined by how long you worked, how much you earned, and your age at retirement. They can also be based on your husband's benefits. Social Security benefits must be applied for; they are not automatically issued.

Benefits can begin at age sixty-two, but a woman who considers this option should balance the value of receiving Social Security income before age sixty-five with the advantages of waiting until age sixty-five to receive a larger benefit. The average benefit paid in 1992 to retired women, based on their own earnings, was $562 per month or $6,744 per year. The maximum annual benefit for a person who retired in 1993 at age sixty-five was $13,536.

If you have not yet begun to receive Social Security benefits and you may be eligible, contact the Social Security Administration to request a free personalized benefits estimate. Call 1-800-772-1213 or a local Social Security office.

Supplemental Security Income

Supplemental Security Income is the federal cash assistance program for the aged, disabled, and blind. The eligibility requirements, based on income and assets, are stringent and differ from state to state. Anyone eligible for SSI may also be eligible for Medicaid, food stamps, and local programs such as housing subsidies. More information about SSI can also be obtained by calling 1-800-772-1213 or a local Social Security office.

Pensions

The traditional pension—paid into by an employer over long years of employment, then paid out on a monthly basis to the retired employee until death—is fading fast and becoming increasingly rare outside government employment. This is especially true for women. In 1992, only about one-fifth of women sixty-five and older received pension benefits, compared to nearly half of men.

Women lack pensions for a variety of reasons. They may have worked in jobs that did not offer benefits. They may have lost their benefits by switching jobs or taking time off to care for family members, or they may have earned too little to be able to contribute to voluntary savings plans. However, if you are entitled to benefits from an employer-sponsored pension—either on your own work record or as a widow or former wife—you need to know what pension benefits are due you and how to make decisions about those benefits. Contact the benefits plan administrator or personnel office of the company where the pension was earned for a copy of the plan's Summary Plan Description and information about the plan. Some companies offer informational seminars for employees. Inquire about these.

A variety of voluntary retirement savings plans have become available to employees, but these were not widely available during the careers of most women who are now over sixty. All of these plans allow money to grow, untaxed, until it is withdrawn at retirement. Most commonly, these plans are: IRAs (individual retirement accounts), SEP-IRAs (IRAs to which an employer contributes), 401(k)s or 401(b)s (employer-sponsored investment programs), Keoghs (investment programs for the self-employed), or ESOPs (employee stock ownership plans).

Savings and Financial Investments

Most financial advisors suggest keeping some money (three- to six-months' living expenses) in an account that is immediately available for emergency expenses. Such advice is easy to give, but often difficult or impossible for women on fixed and limited incomes to follow. In addition to an emergency fund, even a limited one, you may have saved money that provides a financial resource for special expenses or that supplements fixed retirement income from Social Security and pensions. You probably want savings and investments to be secure, yet available for withdrawal when needed.

Some women have developed considerable skill in managing investments. Others regard the process with dread or anxiety. But whether we have very little money or a great deal, as we age we tend to feel increasingly vulnerable to the fear of taking risks with money. We are no longer replenishing our savings with the salaries we once had.

We worry about our money running out in the event that we incur health and long-term care expenses. We also feel anxious about managing our money because we often simply lack the information, experience, and confidence that we need. To turn over our financial affairs to another family member, or to a broker, banker, attorney, accountant, or financial planner, is one option. There are good and compelling reasons to do this if another person is more qualified and competent than we are.

Saving and investing offer different levels of risk and reward. A key rule is that the greater the return sought, the greater the risk. Therefore, a high risk or conservative strategy should be determined by whether you can accept the loss of your investment. Some types of investments are federally insured, but most are not. Be cautious about signing anything you don't understand completely.

The special language of the investment world can be intimidating, but the woman who wishes to enhance her ability to manage and control her money can learn to be responsible for her own financial affairs, even if another trusted person is involved.

Insurance

The purpose of insurance is to protect income and assets or to provide money for beneficiaries. We are required by law to carry insurance on a car or property, but other types of insurance coverage are optional. For most older women, health insurance (usually Medicare or Medicaid), Medigap (Medicare supplement insurance), and long-term care coverage are the most essential. However, long-term care insurance presents a special dilemma. Do you need it? Can you afford it? Is it worth the cost?

Life insurance is designed to build cash values or provide cash benefits to beneficiaries. Insurance companies offer policies to serve a variety of needs. Term insurance, for example, builds no cash value and is payable at your death, and if you drop it, you get nothing back. Other types of life insurance, such as whole life and annuities, accrue cash values.

At this stage of life it is important to carefully review your insurance coverage (and your husband's if you are married). Make sure you understand each policy, its costs, its benefits, and its beneficiaries. Does your insurance coverage provide for your actual needs, can you afford it, and is the insurance company secure and dependable? For example, if you no longer have dependents, you may want only a small policy to cover your burial expenses. Other types of insurance may or may not fit your circumstances.

Employment

Is it worth it to work? Working for pay after age sixty can be necessary for economic survival. It can also be a valuable way to contribute your skills and energy to work that offers a sense of value and self-respect. But for most older women, entering or remaining in the labor force is not an option. Efforts to include older women in the workforce are largely isolated and confined to low-paying, temporary, or part-time work. In fact, in 1993 only 8 percent of women over sixty-five were working, compared to 16 percent of men. These issues are discussed in depth in chapter five.

If paid employment is an option, rather than a necessity, what are the implications of the income you receive? Is it worth it financially? Money you earn may be intended to supplement Social Security, which for millions of older women is their principal income, but be sure to calculate the real value of your paycheck and understand its impact. There is an earnings test that reduces benefits if you are under age seventy. Currently, for women sixty-two to sixty-five, benefits are reduced $1 for every $2 of earnings over $8,640 of annual income. For women sixty-five to sixty-nine, benefits are reduced by $1 for every $3 of earnings over $13,500 of annual income. What is your real income after the cost of working is deducted (taxes, commuting, food, clothing, and so on)? This question is especially critical for women because they are much more likely than men to take marginal jobs in their later years. (For information and assistance with these issues, contact the agencies listed under General Information and Assistance in the resources section of this book.)

Older women may want to choose self-employment rather than enter a hostile and competitive job market. Creating your own work can fulfill a life dream or present a new challenge resulting in personal benefits far more valuable than the income it generates. Although the risk of failure in creating a new business venture is high, maturity and experience may balance the scales with unexpected rewards.

Home Equity

Owning a home when we are over sixty can be both a blessing and a curse. Where we live, with whom, and under what circumstances can be puzzling questions, but the financial questions are especially important when your home is a substantial part of your net worth, a significant expense, or a potential financial resource.

In order to make financial decisions about your home, you need to know what it costs you to live there. Mortgage payments, taxes, insurance, upkeep, repairs, utilities, and other costs are the most common ones. If your financial resources are adequate to support your current lifestyle, you can afford to be sentimental about your house. However, it still makes sense to know what your financial options are in order to plan realistically for your future. The first step in becoming informed about financial options of home ownership is to become familiar with some basic terms.

- *Home equity* is the sale price minus any mortgages.

- *Basis* is what you paid for your house, plus improvements.

- *A capital gains tax* is paid when your house is sold, based on the selling price less basis.

- *A reverse annuity mortgage* is a mortgage on your home that pays the homeowner a certain amount for a period of years.

Housing issues and options are discussed more fully in chapter four.

How Can You Expand Your Income?

Social Security, pensions, savings, investments, insurance, employment, and home equity provide most, but not all, of the income sources for older women. An inheritance, marrying someone with financial assets that they are willing to share, or receiving services or support from family and friends, community, or church may also help to stretch our income.

Simply economizing often forces us to think creatively about our lifestyle and our priorities and to reflect on what really matters to us. Looking for ways to enjoy life while reducing the amount of money we spend is no disgrace. Taking advantage of senior discounts, offering personal services to people instead of expensive gifts, reading books from the library instead of buying them, and discovering that pleasure can come from a walk in the park instead of shopping at the mall can add unexpected benefits to life.

It is worth remembering that financial resources are not limited to money. Although most books on financial management and investment contain charts and instructions for filling in the blanks with dollar amounts, numbers simply don't tell the whole story of our financial lives. Our personal attitudes, skills, and resourcefulness can balance the financial scales in the direction of increased satisfaction rather than despair. Our ability to locate and use community or family resources is a valuable economic factor that does not appear on any net worth statement.

If we have adequate housing, food, and health care, our quality of life depends less on the amount of money we have and more on our own ability to care for ourselves. Any older woman who has experienced a major economic depression, wartime rationing and hardship, marriage, motherhood, divorce, widowhood, job insecurity, mortgages, and other economic challenges knows that despite our best efforts, few can expect to live without having to worry about making ends meet. But even when income is limited, life can be inwardly rich.

How Can You Plan Ahead?

After you have a picture of what you have, what you owe, and what your current income and expenses are, the next step toward financial literacy involves getting organized and planning for the future.

Consider these questions:

* What lifestyle and pattern of spending can you expect for the next year, for five years, for the rest of your life?

* What changes would you like to make now or in the future?

* What changes might you have to make because of illness, widowhood, or family needs?

* What plans do you want to make for your survivors?

One of the keys to a healthy financial future is the ability to confront one's current status and to make wise decisions and choices. This means assembling and organizing personal records, becoming educated, knowing exactly what will happen when we or a partner dies, and setting priorities for the future. Locate all the information you or someone else would need to understand your personal and financial status and plans. These records, especially property deeds, a will, trust, or power of attorney, should be safe, accessible, and conveniently located with copies of important information in more than one place. The location of a safety deposit box key is also important to share with another person. A helpful guide for getting organized is *A Primer on Personal Money Management for Midlife and Older Women* (available free from the AARP).

Estate planning, wills, and probate offer ways to plan for our survivors. Whatever our financial assets, we usually wish to have some control over their dispersal after our death. Waiting too long or just worrying without taking action gives away our power to other family members or to strangers in the legal system. Since four out of five older women will outlive their husbands, basic information about wills and trusts and how to use them is of great importance for women.

No matter how small or large an estate, practical steps can be taken to protect hard-earned assets from unnecessary and excessive taxes and probate costs, and to make sure an estate goes to those we choose. Even modest belongings and assets cannot be given away informally after death. All states have rules governing intestate succession (the process by which an estate is distributed to the heirs if there has been no will or will substitute). We have not only the opportunity, but the responsibility to provide for those we love by making sure our affairs are in order to carry out our wishes.

This section is not meant to replace or duplicate the general estate planning guides that are already widely available, but to highlight the basic issues and questions that need to be examined when planning ahead. Whether you plan to write your own will or to get advice from professionals such as lawyers, financial planners, or tax specialists, consider the following critical issues:

- Declare the *beneficiary(ies)* of each of your assets. The laws in your state covering common-law or community property will affect your planning. In the forty-one common-law property states, assets belong to the spouse whose earnings acquired it. In the nine community property states, each spouse also acquires assets through the efforts of the other.

- Determine whether a *will,* a *trust,* or a combination of both is best suited to your needs. If you or your husband already have a will or a trust, is it up-to-date and have you seen it? Do you understand and approve of its provisions?

  Basically, a *will* is a legal document that states how all of your property should be distributed and names an executor. The provisions of the will become effective when you die. A will usually must go through the probate process (a legal procedure for settling an estate that is supervised by the court and that can take up to two years). The decedent's estate pays all related legal costs (these can be up to 10 percent of the estate).

  A *trust* is a legal arrangement in which you place property "in trust" for the benefit of one or more individuals or an organization. A trust is established by a written agreement in which you name someone (the trustee) to manage assets placed in trust and give instructions on how to distribute the assets. A trust can outline your wishes in detail.

  Living trusts can avoid the delays and cost of probate, and may reduce or eliminate estate taxes. On the other hand, the initial cost of setting up a trust is usually higher than making a will.

- Select a lawyer that you respect and trust to advise you about legal decisions and their consequences for you and your survivors. Many attorneys offer low-cost consultations. Legal Aid, Legal Assistance for Seniors, and other community services are also available for those with limited financial resources.

- Arrange for someone you trust (an attorney, advisor, or family member) to make financial decisions on your behalf if you should become incompetent. A *durable power of attorney* is a written document that authorizes a particular person to perform certain acts on your behalf. A durable power of attorney for health care (a legal document covering health care decisions) is discussed in the chapters on caregiving and health.

Where Can You Look for Help and Information?

None of us is completely alone. We may have many or few close family members, friends, and advisors, but often there are more sources of information and support available to us than we are aware of. Managing one's finances is an ongoing process, not a one-day event. Initially, the work and time involved in getting all the pieces organized and under control may seem to be a world-class task. Yet the freedom, independence, and personal satisfaction you can gain by actively managing your finances far outweigh the risks of doing nothing.

Competent advisors and sources of information are now widely available. Local senior centers, senior service agencies, community colleges, YWCAs, libraries, and other organizations often provide workshops and seminars on estate planning, Medicare and Medigap, long-term care, and other issues. Many TV and radio talk shows and magazine and newspaper articles offer information and advice about money.

Free or low-cost publications are available from the AARP and the Older Women's League. Some of these are listed in the resource section at the end of this book.

Financial institutions, real-estate firms, legal services, and tax advisors help people with specific problems, but their "free" advice may promote the products and services they sell. Be cautious about following the advice of anyone who makes money from your money!

TOWARD FINANCIAL EMPOWERMENT

If you feel daunted by the subject of finances, you're not alone. Midlife and older women—especially those whose marital status has changed or who have had limited paid work experience—are likely to have had little financial education. But you don't need an advanced degree to achieve financial literacy. Increasing our money management skills can strengthen our confidence in making all kinds of decisions, thus enhancing our feelings of empowerment in many areas of our lives.

PERSONAL ASSETS WORKSHEET

Date:————————————

Personal Assets	Type of Ownership	Self	Spouse	Total
Financial Assets				
Cash				
Checking accounts				
Savings accounts				
Certificates of deposit				
Money-market accounts				
Stocks				
Bonds				
Mutual funds				
Money owed you				
Life insurance cash value				
Other				
Retirement Funds				
IRA accounts				
Keogh funds				
Pensions, profit sharing				
Social Security (annual benefits)				
Other				
Property				
Home equity				
Other real estate				
Automobiles				
Household furnishings				
Collectibles				
Other				
Total Value of Personal Assets				

NET WORTH WORKSHEET

Date:_____

Personal Assets	Type of Ownership	Self	Spouse	Total
Financial Liabilities				
Home mortgage				
Other mortgages				
Automobile loans				
Credit card accounts				
Installment accounts				
Personal loans owed				
Taxes owed				
Loans against insurance				
Other				
Total Value of Liabilities				
Total Value of Personal Assets				
Less Total Value of Liabilities				
Total Net Worth				

ANNUAL INCOME AND EXPENSES WORKSHEET

Date from:_____ to:_____

Cash Flow Statement	Self	Spouse	Total
Income (annual) Salary/wages Social Security Pension/retirement Interest/dividends Other			
Total Annual Income			
Expenses (annual) Housing —Mortgage/rent —Utilities —Taxes and insurance —Maintenance Work expenses Life insurance Food —Groceries —Restaurants Transportation Health care —Insurance —Other Debt payments Federal, state, and local taxes Clothing —Laundry and dry cleaning Personal services —Accounting, legal, and other help Recreation and entertainment —Travel and education Gifts and charitable donations Savings Miscellaneous			
Total Annual Expenses			

Chapter Four

HOME IS WHERE THE HEART IS:
Facing Housing Choices

The ideal of happiness has always taken material form in the house,
whether cottage or castle; it stands for permanence and separation
from the world.
—Simone de Beauvoir

HOME IS WHERE THE heart is, There's no place like home, A
woman's home is her castle, Make yourself at home. These time-worn
phrases reflect that where we live affects us deeply. Home is an
expression of our selves, a large part of who we are. The furniture is
familiar and comfortable. We know where everything is. Our possessions bring back memories: the easy chair bought when we were first
married and somehow never replaced, the clay hand imprint on the
wall of the kindergarten grandchild now entering college, the sculp-
ture we bought on vacation and struggled to take home on the plane.
We may have tended our garden lovingly for years and seen a seedling
grow into a shady tree. Our home links us to our neighborhood and
community. We know where to find things on the grocery shelves,
which stores have the best values, and which is the best cleaner to
use. We feel comfortable in our church, temple, or any group that we
belong to, or we are often looked to as an informal historian.

According to a recent AARP survey, 84 percent of older people
want to stay in their own homes for the rest of their lives. That is true
whether the home is a one-bedroom cottage, a walk-up apartment, or

a large three-bedroom house in the suburbs. Leaving a home we have lived in for a long time is seen as a major loss that affects the rest of our lives. When personal, financial, and physical changes make staying in our homes problematic, our first choice is to find ways to adapt the home so we can continue living there. Failing that, we want to locate housing alternatives that duplicate, to the greatest extent possible, the values of privacy, safety, and comfort that our home typified.

Life changes that affect housing may come at any time. What will you do if your husband has a stroke and dies, and your daughter wants you to sell the house and move in with her? Or the stroke doesn't result in death, but prolonged disability. How will you decide whether you could care for him at home? Or what if your mobility becomes impaired? What changes could you make in your home and what services could you bring into the home to make it possible for you to care for a disabled spouse or be cared for there yourself? Now that your children have left home, does your house feel too empty, too big, and too much of a drain on your financial resources? Have you or your husband recently retired, and are you thinking about what you want to do with all that leisure time? Is this an opportunity to make some positive changes in your lifestyle by moving into a different kind of community? Have there been changes in the neighborhood that make you consider moving, such as the closing of favorite stores or restaurants, feeling less safe walking the streets, or friends moving away or dying?

Advanced planning helps you feel more competent and in control. You can explore your options while you have the time and energy and without the stress of an emergency situation. This chapter will help you assess your current situation and anticipate what may lie ahead. It offers suggestions and describes how a home might be adapted to enable you to stay where you are, and how home equity can become a source of income. Issues about sharing your home with relatives or others are also discussed. The final section presents a guide to housing alternatives if it becomes necessary to move on.

How Well Is Your Home Working for You Now?

Look around your home with a fresh perspective and consider whether it is a safe, comfortable, and affordable place to live. Are there simple ways to improve it?

* Does its size suit you, even though there may be rooms you are not using at present?

* Is it easy for you to get in and out of the house, or do you have difficulty climbing stairs? Could you install a handrail?

* Are your major appliances in working order? If not, are they worth repairing? Can you afford to replace them?

* Can you prepare meals easily in your kitchen? Should you consider having your main meal prepared for you through a service like Meals on Wheels or by ordering take-out?

* Are snow removal or yard care becoming a burden? Are there teenagers you could hire or family members who would do it for you?

* Are utility and maintenance costs within your budget? Is there anything you could do to reduce them, such as shutting off the heat in rooms you are not using and turning off lights when you leave a room? Are you eligible for financial assistance?

If you own your home:

* Is it in need of major repairs, that is, what is the condition of the roof, and how old are the furnace and hot water heater? Do you want to consider drawing on your home's equity for home improvements? (See the section on home equity loans later in this chapter.) Or could you get financial assistance if needed?

* Are property taxes and other assessments manageable? Does

your community have a program for reduced or deferred taxes for older homeowners?

If you are renting:

* If you are not on the ground floor, is there a reliable elevator? Would it accommodate a wheelchair? Are the controls reachable from a wheelchair?

* Do you have a long-term lease, with limitations on rent increases? Could the lease be terminated in the event of the death or incapacity of you or your husband?

Characteristics of your neighborhood and community should also be considered. Think about which of these or other factors are important to you:

* Does the neighborhood feel safe when you are walking around or driving? Is it adequately policed?

* Are there neighbors and friends who can help if you need it?

* Is public transportation readily available? Does it run frequently to parts of town you regularly use for shopping, for medical and dental care, and for visiting with friends?

* Are there shopping and service facilities such as a market, laundry, bank, post office, or library within walking distance, or are they accessible by public transportation?

A basic issue is whether you can afford to stay in your present home. Whether you rent or own, it is possible to reduce your utility costs. Programs may be supported by state or local governments and by local utility companies. These include subsidies, budgeting programs to spread the costs evenly over the entire year, and free or low-cost weatherization programs to cut your heating and air-conditioning bills.

Contact your local utility company, state public utility commission, or local Area Agency on Aging to learn what's available in your area.

If you are a home owner, this chapter discusses possible ways to use your home equity to provide you with monthly income. Many states have provisions for reduced or deferred property taxes, and local communities sometimes establish special programs to provide no-cost or low-cost home repair services to older homeowners. Availability and eligibility criteria vary greatly for all of these programs. Check with your Area Agency on Aging and local planning board to learn what exists in your community.

If you are a renter, this chapter describes Section 8 assistance, a federally funded rental assistance program. There are, however, often long waiting lists for acceptance into this program.

ADAPTING YOUR HOME IN ANTICIPATION OF FUTURE NEEDS

You may want to make some changes now in anticipation of diminished sight, hearing, mobility, or short-term illness or disability. Minor adjustments can make your house safer.

* Check for poor lighting, especially in long halls and on stairways. Use higher-watt bulbs. Install night lights with automatic light sensors in bathrooms, hallways, the kitchen, and entryways. Purchase a light that goes on automatically at the clap of hands for your entrance hall. Make sure there is a light switch at the top and bottom of each staircase as well as throughout the house.

* Clear pathways of furniture. Remove or secure throw rugs! Tape electric cords to the walls. Keep newspapers and other clutter away from walking areas.

* Make sure staircases have handrails that are sturdy and easy to grasp. Place nonskid strips on stairs. Light-colored strips make the edge of the stairs more visible. You can purchase adhesive-

backed tape in most hardware stores.

- Install grab bars that are bolted to the bathtub or shower. Use a handheld showerhead so you can sit while bathing. If you bathe in a shower without a tub, add a nonskid shower seat. Put a nonskid mat or strips in the bathtub or shower.

- Grab bars next to the toilet are also helpful. They should be secured to the wall studs.

- Lower the thermostat on the hot water heater to 120 degrees to prevent scalding. Your gas company can do this for you.

Other simple alterations can make living easier:

- Modify furniture. For those who are taller, raise the bed a few inches to make it easier to get in and out. Drawers with a single pull are easier to open. Firmer, straight-back furniture is easier to get in and out of. Buy lamps with easy on and off switches or those that go on and off with a clap of the hands.

- Install large lever-type controls on faucets, door latches, and appliance knobs.

- Add electrical outlets and a phone jack that are accessible to your bed.

- If your bedrooms are upstairs, consider whether a downstairs room might be used as a bedroom if necessary.

An excellent reference for home adaptation is *The Do-able Renewable Home,* published by the AARP.

HOME OWNERSHIP AS A POSSIBLE SOURCE OF INCOME

The biggest single investment most people make is their home. Eighty percent of older homeowners have built up large equities in their homes and are now making no or low mortgage payments. At the same time, they may have monthly incomes that do not meet their financial needs. Large expenses for home maintenance or health care may be causing economic hardship. A sudden change such as the death of a spouse or loss of an income source can result in home mortgage delinquencies and danger of foreclosure.

There are now a number of ways under the general heading of home equity conversion that allow homeowners to transform their accumulated equity into cash or a regular monthly income. They fall into two main categories: home equity loans and reverse mortgages.

Home Equity Loans

A home equity loan is essentially a second mortgage on your home. The funds can be received either in a lump sum or drawn upon as needed. Interest rates are usually lower than for consumer loans or credit card borrowing, and the repayment terms can be much longer. *There are real dangers,* however, and you should *never* take out a home equity loan unless you are *sure* you can make all the payments on time. If you miss payments, the lender has the automatic right to foreclose and put your house up for sale to the highest bidder. You would probably not get a fair market value and could be evicted from your home like any tenant who failed to pay rent.

Reverse Mortgages

Reverse mortgages work like any other mortgage, but instead of receiving a sum of money that you must then start repaying in monthly installments, you get money that doesn't have to be repaid until either the end of the loan term, when you move, when you sell the house, or when you die. Some reverse mortgages now will continue to provide lifetime income even though you no longer live in the home. The money can be paid to you in a lump sum or in installments. These usually consist of monthly payments for a specified period or until the borrower's death or the sale of the home. No income tax is paid on monthly advances. Principal and interest charges accumulate until the loan is due. The amount available to you depends on your age and the value of your home. Lenders will generally lend up to 80 percent of the home's value.

The use of reverse mortgages should be looked at as an option if you are "shelter poor," that is, if you have money tied up in your home and not enough cash to live comfortably. Nearly 25 percent of low-income older homeowners have at least $50,000 equity in their homes. Almost 75 percent of poor single homeowners age seventy-five and over could raise their income above the poverty line by converting home equity into income.

Loans insured by the Federal Housing Administration are available in most states. Potential borrowers must be over sixty-two, have little or no outstanding mortgage, and maintain the home as their principal residence for the duration of the reverse mortgage. If the homeowner moves, the mortgage becomes due and payable. The Federal National Mortgage Association ("Fannie Mae") has launched its own reverse mortgage program, the Home Keeper Mortgage, across the country. Its entry into the market will vastly expand the number of reverse mortgages available.

Caution. There are also major problems. Reverse mortgages usually cost more than standard mortgages. There is great variation in the fees charged by different financial institutions, and some may be exorbitant. Loan origination fees might run 1 or 2 percent of the loan amount. There can also be appraisal fees, service fees, and exit fees at the time of the sale. A county in California recently filed a class action suit against one of the nation's biggest insurance companies, charging it with defrauding senior citizens by charging excessive fees on those reverse mortgages.

Other factors to check into are the financial health and stability of the company making the loan and the flexibility to make changes in the program if your needs change. Most reverse mortgages require that the home be sold to repay the mortgage when the homeowner dies. This means you could not will it to your inheritors. Some have the requirement that the house must be sold if the homeowner is in a nursing home for more than a year.

Reverse mortgages are complex financial instruments. The AARP and the National Center for Home Equity Conversion have valuable publications to help you analyze your choices. (See Resources.) If you are considering a reverse mortgage, you should consult an attorney or Legal Assistance for Seniors before proceeding. Free counseling about reverse mortgages is also available from your state's Department of Aging.

An alternative you may want to discuss with your children or other family members is whether they are in a position to provide you with monthly payments against their eventual ownership of your home. If you do this, you should consult an attorney to draw up a legal document specifying the terms of the agreement, just as you would for any other legal contract.

LIVING ALONE OR IN SHARED HOUSING

The most likely decision you will have to make about your housing is whether to continue living there alone. You may find yourself suddenly alone at the death of a husband, partner, or companion, or there may be a change in your physical condition that raises questions about the advisability of your present living arrangements.

Residing Alone

Elder women are much more likely than elder men to live alone. Forty-two percent of all women sixty-five or older lived alone in 1992, compared to only 16 percent of men that age. Women's chances of living alone increase as they age: 34 percent of women sixty-five to seventy-four and 52 percent of those seventy-five and older. In 1993, for those sixty-five and older, 75 percent of men were married and living with their wives, while only 41 percent of women were married and living with their husbands.

Living arrangements also differ significantly by ethnic group. Older whites are only half as likely to live with relatives as older African-Americans or Hispanics—12 percent for whites compared to 24 percent for African-Americans and 26 percent for Hispanics.

Moving to a New Location

You may want to continue living alone, but in a new home. If we live in the chilly north, there is the lure of the Sun Belt and the thought of no more snow to shovel. The idea of living near, but not with, children and grandchildren may be appealing and reassuring. In making such a decision, it is important to think about both what you would be giving up and what you would be gaining.

You would be leaving not only your own home, as would be true in moving to any new housing arrangement, but your community. Community in this sense consists of places, but more importantly it refers to the friendships and relationships that can give our lives meaning. And as discussed earlier, there is the comfort of the familiar, of knowing how to get where you want to go and what you'll find when you get there.

On the other hand, you may be challenged by a new move and feel that it would be an adventure to see and do different things. Or your neighborhood may have changed, friends moved away or died, and you no longer feel comfortable living there.

Before making a decision about a new location, try to visit it a number of times and, if possible, at different times of the year. If you are thinking about buying a home, you might want to rent or sublease an apartment in that area first. Before making a decision you should find out the following:

- What is the cost of living? What are the state and local taxes, housing costs, and other basic expenses?

- What medical facilities are available? Are there convenient doctors and specialists who accept Medicare, hospitals and nursing homes, home health services?

- What is the environment? Do you like the climate? Is there a problem with pollution?

- Is public transportation available to the places you will want to go? Are taxi vouchers or medical vans available?

- Are there nearby stores, restaurants, laundry, repair, banking, and other services?

- Are there recreational and cultural facilities that you might enjoy such as parks, a swimming pool, golf courses, movie theaters, live theater, concert halls, museums, or social activities through senior centers, a community center, or local service clubs? Are there educational opportunities through a local college, adult high school, or library? Is there a local church or temple of your choice?

Home Sharing

If you are presently living alone and not happy about it, or if you want to prepare yourself for that eventuality, there are various alternatives to consider. Sharing a home—either someone moving into your home or you moving in with someone else—with another person or a group may seem at first glance to be the easiest and most practical solution. To make it work, however, requires being very clear about mutual needs and expectations. Various patterns of home sharing include:

- living with a child or other relative

- living with one or more nonrelated persons

- building separate living quarters on your property

- moving into a group household

- joining a program that will match you with others looking for shared housing

Adding an Accessory Apartment

You might want the security and assistance of someone nearby, without sharing your actual living quarters. Or you might be looking for additional sources of income. If you own your home and the property is large enough, you could add a separate self-contained unit, referred to as an accessory apartment (often called a "mother-in-law" apartment). You would need to determine first whether zoning regulations permit such an addition. A number of localities are making exceptions, allowing older homeowners to build accessory apartments. You would have to consider whether the costs of renovation and other possible increased expenses, such as higher taxes or insurance, are worth the added income or assistance. It is also a very time-consuming and trying process. You would have to obtain the necessary permits, select and work with a contractor, and arrange for financing. You would also need to feel comfortable in the role of landlord. That means not only going through the process of keeping the property rented (advertising, interviewing, credit and reference checks, and so on), but being responsible for anything that might go wrong with the apartment.

Living with Relatives

Living with adult children or relatives can be particularly difficult because of the history you share and the complex interrelationships that already exist. As other options have become available and families have become less able to accommodate a parent, fewer elders are living with relatives. However, if members can reach common understandings about the basics of living together, multigenerational families can work well and enrich the lives of all concerned. A loving grandmother can give support and understanding to a grandchild and offer help with child care to harried parents. The life experiences of an older woman can lend perspective to the demands of today's world. Living with adult children can broaden a parent's horizons.

When your child or other relative urges you to move in, they may be primarily expressing feelings of worry and concern about your welfare, particularly if it is at a time of crisis. They may not have thought about what it would mean in terms of day-to-day living. Your feelings of gratitude for this support may also prevent you from assessing the idea in realistic terms.

The most important factor in the success or failure of sharing a home with your child is the ability of the two of you to sit down and frankly discuss how your living together would change your relationship. If your child is married, it is also important to include your daughter- or son-in-law in any discussion. You would need to see each other as adult partners in decision making about the household and anticipate how you would handle problems as they would arise. So it is necessary for *each* of you to be as clear as you can be about potential arrangements:

- How would the living space be divided?

- Would you be taking a room in the other person's home, or would you be sharing the home equally?

- How would living expenses be shared?

- What would be each person's responsibility for household chores?

It is also important to discuss how much and what kind of help you would need and expect from your child or relative:

- How much time do you expect your child or relative to spend with you? How does that fit with the other demands on their time from work, children, and social life?

- Will you need assistance with activities of daily living, such as dressing, grooming, or eating? Are they willing and able to provide this level of care? If not, can you or they afford to hire this kind of assistance?

- Are you able to drive or use public transportation? If not, are they willing to provide you with transportation? Do they have daytime hours available? Can you make other provisions through a van or taxi service to get to needed medical appointments and other places you want to go?

Another factor to consider, particularly if moving in means moving away from your neighborhood, is the degree to which you will be dependent on your family to provide you with social support. How will you keep up your present friendships if they will no longer be living close to you? Can you arrange for less frequent but longer visits? Can you make more frequent, regular phone contact?

Will you be leaving your religious organization, senior center, or any other group that is important to you? Would similar organizational connections be available to you in your new location?

How can your family help you to make new social connections? Do they have friends with parents your age they might introduce to you? Can one of them go with you on your first visit to a new organization or group?

There are bound to be differences in lifestyle that can cause friction, such as noise levels, bedtimes, needs for privacy, or tastes in music or TV. What happens when one of you is entertaining friends? If there are grandchildren in the household, will you be able to accept the parents' right to set the rules and determine discipline, even when you disagree? What about your tolerance for the commotion children bring to a home?

Living with Unrelated People

If you decide to share housing with one or more nonrelated people, you would still have to deal with issues of mutual needs and expectations, but without the same level of emotional involvement. You would have to spend enough time together to determine whether you and your prospective housemate(s) are compatible. You would also need to check with your local zoning or planning board to make sure that the zoning regulations permit two or more nonrelated people to share a household.

A shared household may be set up with the expenses and responsibilities for the household divided equally. If someone will be moving into your home, you can exchange specified services for a reduction in rent. Such arrangements are popular with college students and other young people. It is important to be very clear, in writing, about what is required: how many hours per day or week of housekeeping assistance, meal preparation, shopping, or personal services in exchange for rent or a specified percentage reduction of rent. You should declare how much notice is required by each of you to terminate the arrangement.

Matched Housing

According to the Shared Housing Resource Center, there are over five hundred agencies that provide a matching service for people looking for shared housing. Many of these are connected to religious organizations, social service agencies, or senior centers. There may be a matching of people with varying degrees of disability or frailty. The concept is to put together a group of people who can function as an extended family, helping and supporting each other. Group residences may offer meals, housekeeping, and transportation. Some that cater to disabled or frail residents are connected to social agencies that provide a resident manager or staff support. The Shared Housing Resource Center (see Resources) can give you information about shared housing available in your community.

Setting Up Your Own Group Housing

You and a group of friends who share the same circumstances, that is, living alone and not liking it, may decide to look for housing together. Or you might use the services of a senior center or social agency to locate others interested in communal living. The Shared Housing Resource Center can give you helpful information.

This could mean finding a house to rent or buy. If possible, it is advisable to rent first, until you are sure you are comfortable with your housemates and the living arrangement. If you are considering joint ownership, get expert legal advice about how to set up the title arrangements.

A relatively new form of communal living is called co-housing. In this model each individual or couple has a private house or apartment, and they share common facilities, which usually include a dining room, kitchen, and living room. In order to afford the common space, the individual dwellings are usually 10 to 15 percent smaller than average. Residents manage and maintain the development jointly. Since few existing buildings are suitable for co-housing, it usually involves new buildings or extensive renovations to an existing structure. In Emeryville, California, for example, a group of people of mixed ages, both single and in couples, are converting a large warehouse into co-housing.

A significant advantage is that residents create a social network providing mutual help and support. The main disadvantage is the length of time involved in designing and building the housing. Prospective residents usually meet together frequently in the planning stages to forge joint decisions. It is also necessary to spend enough time together as a group before making any commitments to be sure members are compatible. Co-housing arrangements are often started by a group of interested individuals, a social agency or fraternal group, or in a few instances by local city governments.

HOUSING DESIGNED FOR ELDERS

Senior housing and retirement living are two terms for housing designed to meet the special needs of older people. They conjure up very different images. The first may remind us of "old-age homes," dreary and forlorn, with the "old folks" tucked out of the sight or caring of others and left to spend their days staring at TV or at nothing. The second expression may give us an equally stereotyped picture of healthy and hearty "seniors" living carefree lives in well-appointed, comfortable apartments, enjoying the golf course and clubhouse. There are places, of course, that embody each extreme. But what exists today is a variety of alternatives to meet the changing needs of elders. The choices that may fit you will depend on your income, your locality (urban, suburban, or rural), your health (and that of your spouse, if you are married), and whether you are ready to think about long- or short-term plans.

Independent Senior Housing
Housing designed specifically for healthy and independent older people includes a full spectrum from luxurious high-rise apartments and country club estates to modest publicly subsidized apartments.

Federally subsidized housing projects can be run by for-profit developers or nonprofit agencies and organizations. Housing owned and operated by local public housing authorities uses federal grants to finance construction and operating expenses. Over five thousand units of public housing are now occupied by older adults. These have very stringent low-income requirements and long waiting lists. Section 202 housing (referring to that section of the National Housing

Act) operates on similar low-income criteria to provide low-interest loans to nonprofit sponsors, construction grants, and operating subsidies for congregate housing.

The Housing Act of 1974 established the Section 8 federal housing subsidy program. It provides vouchers to qualifying individuals that can be used to subsidize rent payments. Although not specifically targeted at older people, 60 percent of older renters meet the criterion of spending more than 30 percent of their income on rent.

It is estimated that over 1.5 million older adults are served by some form of federal housing subsidy. These multiple, sometimes overlapping, programs are confusing. To determine if you are eligible for housing assistance, contact your regional office of the Housing and Urban Development Agency (HUD) or your local Area Agency on Aging.

Private older adult housing, often referred to as retirement residences or congregate housing, can be just for healthy active adults, in combination with some degree of assisted living, or as part of a life-care community. (Assisted living and life care are topics of the next section.)

Private senior housing tends to be for those with moderate or high incomes. Couples or single elders who own homes that have become too large, expensive, or difficult to maintain may like the alternative of selling their homes to move into smaller apartments, free of the cares of home ownership. Housing can be in high-rise apartment hotels, offering dining-room meals, housekeeping services, transportation, and recreational activities.

Retirement communities are usually on large, landscaped grounds with a number of amenities, including pools, golf courses, clubhouses, classes, and planned activities. Transportation may be provided for medical appointments, shopping, and entertainment. Meals may or may not be offered in a central dining room. Units may be individually owned condominiums or co-ops or may be rented. Condos and co-ops can have tax advantages. It may be difficult, however, to sell your unit when it no longer suits your needs or upon your death. These units don't hold their value as well as single dwellings, and the potential market is limited to those interested in congregate senior housing.

The major consideration about moving into senior housing of any type is whether you like the idea of age-segregated housing. For some, living away from the noise and commotion of young children and with others who are likely to share common interests is very appealing. For others it is appalling.

Assisted Living

Assisted living facilities are also called board and care homes, personal care facilities, or residential care facilities. These situations are a middle ground between living independently and living in a nursing home. They offer care short of skilled nursing. Facilities vary greatly in the specific services offered. They usually provide three meals a day, housekeeping and laundry, and twenty-four-hour staff in the event of emergencies and to assist with personal care. Many of these facilities provide transportation services and planned social activities.

States have different licensing requirements about the kind of assistance with daily living activities that is permitted in assisted living facilities. Some are able to provide help with such activities as eating, dressing, bathing, going to the bathroom, getting in and out of a wheelchair, and supervision of taking medications. In other states, this level of care can only be provided in a life care facility (see the next section) or nursing home. Some states require that the resident be ambulatory and able to leave the facility without assistance in the event of emergency.

Assisted living facilities can be private homes with a few residents or large institutions with a hundred or more inhabitants. The smaller facilities are generally in a residential neighborhood and have more of a home atmosphere. Residents will have meals together in the dining room and gather in the living room for social interaction. Many retirement communities and congregate housing offer assisted living services as an option when the resident first moves in, or if it becomes necessary later.

Costs for assisted living depend on the type of facility, its auspices (private or nonprofit), the accommodations—single room, shared room, suite, or apartment—the locality, and what services are needed. Neither Medicare nor Medicaid pay for assisted living. If you qualify for the Supplemental Security Income federal assistance program, costs may be covered. Some private long-term care insurance now covers assisted living. There is little regulation of assisted living facilities beyond basic licensing by the state; therefore, evaluating quality and the services offered become major issues. It is important to check out a number of facilities before making a decision. The Assisted Living Facilities Association of America promotes the development of high standards for the industry and provides several useful publications. The local office of the long-term care ombudsman, if there is one in your area, can provide lists and information about local licensed facilities. Religious organizations, social agencies, and senior centers often have referral information. Nothing substitutes, however, for on-site inspection. If possible, bring a family member along to provide another opinion. Look at the type of room or accommodation you want to rent as well as the group facilities. Talk to the staff about the services they provide and to residents about how they feel about their care. Review the house rules and make sure they are acceptable to you. When you have narrowed down your choices, visit again. Nursing homes are discussed in chapter six.

Continuing Care Retirement Facilities (CCRCs)

These facilities, also called life care communities, offer services similar to congregate housing but additionally provide a continuum of lifelong care. Most require that you be healthy and able to live independently at the time you move in. Some will accept residents who require limited personal assistance. Then, if your needs change, you can move from the independent living section (your own room or apartment) to the assisted living section (usually a single or double room). A skilled nursing facility will also be available, and you may move in and out of it as your condition requires. Your previous room or apartment may be rented, however, if you are out of it for an extended time, and you may have to wait for a vacancy before you can move back into a lower level of care. Your monthly fees will go up for the time spent in the assisted living or nursing home section.

CCRCs can give you peace of mind, knowing that you have provided for your future and the unpredictable changes in health and abilities that advancing age may bring. They are expensive, however. Most require steep entrance fees, sometimes called "endowment fees," that may be nonrefundable or only partially refundable. Entrance fees can vary from $50,000 to $250,000. These are most often paid for by the proceeds of selling a house. Then there will be monthly fees that vary according to the type of accommodation you choose and the level of care you require. A few CCRCs do not require an entrance fee but have higher monthly fees. Some offer a choice of plans with different levels of endowment fees and monthly fees.

You enter a life care facility under a contractual agreement defining your rights to shelter and services for as long as you are in the facility, and the conditions for the refund of the entrance fee, if any. These are complex documents, and you should review them with an attorney before signing. It is important to understand who makes the decisions about when a resident transfers from one level of care to another, what if any additional fees are involved, and any requirements for health or nursing home insurance. Some facilities are meeting their contractual agreement to provide full nursing home care by requiring residents to purchase long-term care insurance. Others will charge higher fees for nursing home care until the resident has reduced assets to the point of qualifying for Medicaid and will then accept the Medicaid rate. Be alert to possible changes in Medicaid financing for nursing home care that may affect these arrangements.

In choosing a CCRC, you are making a long-term commitment, so the facility's financial health is a concern. Review the facility's financial statement with your accountant, financial advisor, or attorney. Check with your local long-term care ombudsman, if available, and your local Better Business Bureau or Consumer Protection Office, about possible complaints and the facility's disposition. The American Association of Homes for the Aging accredits CCRCs and publishes a list of facilities that have met their standards. It also publishes two good resources: CCRCs: A Guidebook for Consumers and The Consumer's Directory of CCRCs.

LOOKING AHEAD

This chapter has hopefully given you a broader picture of what "home" can mean. If you plan ahead and consider alternatives, you will be more likely to have a greater degree of control over your own life. The resources section will provide you with additional information about agencies and organizations in the housing field. Talk to elders like yourself who may have experience with different living arrangements or who also want to explore housing possibilities. And talk to family members now about some of the what-ifs, so they, too, will be prepared to help you make necessary changes.

Chapter Five

WORK AND BEYOND:
The Retirement Years

To be able to fill leisure intelligently is the
last product of civilization.
—Bertrand Russell

THE "GREYING OF AMERICA" is creating an entirely new problem. In the future our society will be faced with cohort after cohort of
healthy and active people, who on the average will spend one-fifth to
one-third of their lives in retirement. Most of them will be women. In
the past, few people lived long enough to experience a period when
they were no longer in the labor force. Old age came earlier and illnesses took their toll, but people tended to work as long as they had
the strength. Due to demographic and social changes, we are different from previous generations in three major ways: We can expect to
live longer and be healthier; as Social Security pay has become available to a large segment of the over sixty-five population, more of us
can make choices about how to use our remaining years; and the
norms guiding behavior of older people have drastically changed in
the past fifty years.

Instead of being built-in baby-sitters for their children, many
grandparents are now touring the country in RVs and motor homes or

moving into retirement enclaves. The affluent elderly might be buying condos at golf courses or seeing the world from cruise ships and tour buses. Such lifestyles are often portrayed as the most desirable goal for our retirement years, although the truth is that only a small section of the older population can afford it.

Images of grandmothers in rocking chairs have long been passé. The unwritten codes of proper behavior for older women have been relaxed to the point that an older woman can choose any activity that her health, strength, and bankbook permit. She may join groups for dancing, golfing, sailing, mountain climbing, or gambling. If she is single, she can join singles groups and go on dates, and she has a much greater probability of finding a mate and getting married than her mother would have had at the same age.

MEANINGFUL ACTIVITIES IN LATER LIFE

As we move from work to retirement, we might feel that our society thrusts us from one set of values to another set that is diametrically opposite. Productivity, achievement, usefulness, industriousness, and ambition are by and large what our society has expected from us, whether as workers in the labor market or as caretakers of our families. These values have given meaning to our lives as we strived to make our contributions to the focal areas of work and home. Most of our actions have been dictated by a need to add to the promotion and perfection of these realms. Rewards have been there in many forms, and also an increased sense of identity and self-worth. Now our children are raised and our work is done. We are let out through the gate into the green pastures of retired life. Advertisements targeting the retired population market would have us believe that leisure is the ultimate value, the goal we have strived for all our life. After a life governed by a "busy ethic," suggesting we should be busy and our activities should be meaningful, we no longer have a framework on how to spend to our time meaningfully.

Joseph B. Fabry, in his book *The Pursuit of Meaning*, elaborates on Victor Frankl's logotherapy teachings:

> What I gained from logotherapy is the recognition that central to human life is the pursuit of meaning and not the pursuit of happiness, that we only invite frustration if we expect life to be primarily pleasurable, that life imposes obligations, and that pleasure and happiness come from responding to the tasks of life. (p. 6)

Our main motivation for living is not seeking pleasure but self-chosen tasks, and the deepest pleasure comes from accomplishing these tasks. (p. 18)

It follows that activity for activity's sake is not the answer to our quest for meaning. And it is especially important to recognize that the answers are specific for each individual. Having something to do is important, but the task we choose does not have to be determined by its usefulness. We do not necessarily share perceptions of what is meaningful after retirement the way we shared the work ethic. Volunteer work might provide abundant meaning to one person but not to another. An extroverted person may turn to social activities or social activism, an introverted person may turn to activities fulfilling his or her aesthetic or inner life. As we pass through the phases from early retirement and into old age, we should also expect our interests and focus to change.

WHAT WORK MEANS TO WOMEN

In the not-so-distant past, paid work was considered to have different meaning for women than for men. Although women primarily worked only as a response to need, men expected to be fulfilled by their work, and if not by work itself, by the achievement of manhood through work and the breadwinner role. Women's fulfillment came from motherhood and the nurturing and serving role assigned to her by society. The forces that changed the social landscape almost overnight left both men and women with the sometimes dubious freedom of having to define their own preferences vis-à-vis their social and family roles.

As women now have access to more rewarding and better-paying jobs, they are also gaining more satisfaction in their work roles; they are learning not to shun male jobs and to take pride in their accomplishments. There are indications that work has taken on a similar value for women as for men. However, women garner somewhat different benefits and experiences from work than men. Studies indicate that women tend to have more close relationships than men, with a larger social support network. The social ties formed at work provide important support for women, in particular if they are single, whereas men tend to rely on one key relationship, usually the spouse, as his source of support. The workplace offers opportunities to form a supportive circle of friends. Since women are often isolated in suburban neighborhoods, the home is not necessarily the best source for rich community bonds.

It has been a widely held belief that retirement is easier for women. Upon retirement, so it was thought, women could return to their primary role as homemakers without feeling much regret over their loss of the work role. There is now growing evidence that work holds great positive value in women's lives. Available research indicates that women are more likely to want to retire late or to go on working indefinitely, and not only for financial reasons. Work enriches a woman's social life, and women see retirement in a less positive view than men do. This is true in particular for lower-income and single women. Women are more likely than men to plan never to retire, and if they do plan to retire, to retire late. Thus, contrary to common belief, many women have a harder time adjusting to retirement than men, they don't necessarily like retirement, and they might have negative psychological symptoms, especially if faced with retirement before they are ready for it. This can be particularly true for women who have entered the labor market late in life.

If you have been a homemaker and your relationship to the world of work has been mainly through your husband's work role, you are certain to feel the impact of his retirement. You need to be aware of the difficulties that can go with his adjustment to retirement and encourage him to plan for it ahead of time and also to be a part of his planning. You need to be aware of the feelings of loss that your husband might experience and be prepared for ways he will attempt to compensate for such losses.

Transition into Retirement

In its very essence, retirement is different from our earlier transitions. Most of our life transitions have moved toward new goals, new achievements, new challenges. As we move away from the adult, work-oriented middle period of our life, however, we are moving toward a less defined phase in our life cycle, that of retirement, and for most people retirement constitutes the doorway to elderhood; it is the concrete event that confirms that we are moving on in years and that we will have to accept and be comfortable with our elder status.

Still, it is important not to make the event of retirement synonymous with old age. Since retirement tends to have a powerful effect on how society perceives us, we should guard against accepting the labels and stereotypes that prematurely put the stamp of inactive old age on all retired persons even while we are still energetic and active. Aging is a process, it does not happen overnight. There are great individual differences in the way people reach old age.

How we prepare for and weather this transition will determine how we live out the rest of our lives. As we plan for and create a new lifestyle, we will also have to give some thought to how to deal with the stages of diminished strength and activity.

But here guideposts are lacking. Our society offers scant support for this time of our lives, understandably, since in some important respects we are different from previous generations. Earlier, people who reached age sixty or sixty-five did not have to go in search for new roles and worthwhile activities. Roles, although limited, existed and so did a sense of value, as old people were integrated in a family system where they were often needed to do useful work.

What we are offered today are some lifestyle models for decisions and choices, telling us, for example, that we might move to a retirement community, spending the rest of our lives playing golf or doing community service work. But there is little guidance for what is actually involved in redesigning our identities and coping with the many changes and challenges of this time in our lives. Such challenges come in many forms, and are specific for each individual. We must accept that work will no longer provide promotions and a sense of accomplishment.

But there is a positive side. Retirement from work presents an opportunity to create, maybe for the first time in our lives, the kind of lifestyle we desire. Now we are looking forward to many years of independence and freedom from external constraints. It will be up to us to fill our days with activities and events, to make decisions, to realize dreams. We are offered a period in life when we can set our own pace, choose our own activities, enjoy leisure without guilt, develop our dormant talents, and employ our unused skills, all free from the weight of work and family responsibilities. All this new bounty, this freedom from structure, this absence of constraints, expectations, and responsibilities, is now ours to use as we see fit. The challenge here has to do with making the choices that will help us adjust to this new stage in our lives. Hectic activities are not necessarily the answer; there's a deeper need to come to terms with and be at peace with the limitations of human life—letting go. This does not happen overnight.

What Will You Miss When You Retire?

We might go through life without being acutely aware of the deep psychological needs we have—as long as they are filled. Many of these needs are partly satisfied by the work we do, the organization we work for, or the people we work with. We might not realize until afterward how important their fulfillment is to our well-being. These needs are not equally important to everyone, but thinking about some of them might help you decide how important your job is to you, and what you might miss when you leave it. Work gives us identity; it structures our days. We have to meet goals and expectations at work that add to our achievements. The workplace is a territory that we feel is our turf. Some might derive power and influence from their jobs, and most importantly, we often relate to a group of people that gives a sense of belonging.

Questions to Ask When Considering Early Retirement

For many people the decision of when to retire is often an agonizing one. For all those who are eagerly looking forward to their retirement day, there may be equally as many who are wrestling with the decision, and understandably so. The relationship to work and the workplace is of overarching importance during an individual's working life, and since work defines people more than almost anything else, the question of when to end this relationship is not to be taken lightly. Early retirement can be a mistake, and it usually cannot be reversed.

The following questions will help you focus on the important facts you need to consider before making a decision about early retirement.

+ Do you have a choice about retirement?

+ What is your motivation for retiring?

+ What lifestyle do you desire?

- Can you afford to retire?

- Are you clear about what work means to you? Do you like or dislike your work?

- Is your spouse/partner in complete agreement with your retirement plans?

- Should you work after you retire?

- Is your estate in order?

When Husbands Retire

Wives are often included in their husbands' pension plans and retirement benefits and therefore feel protected financially. But the economic consequences of the joint or separate retirement of both spouses can turn out to be negative for women. (See chapter three.) If you plan to retire when your husband retires, your combined financial situation should be examined. It is important to be clear as to what your financial situation will be in the event of your husband's death or a divorce.

Family Problems

Marital relations after retirement are rarely seen as problematic and tend to be overlooked in the preparation for retirement. For women who have been full-time homemakers, the husband's retirement can be a drastic change. It can be the beginning of a better and richer relationship with time for each other, but it can also mean a difficult adjustment period. He is dealing with problems of losses of work, status, and turf. You are seeing your freedom limited by his needs for company and for activities. He has lost his turf; you see your turf invaded by him.

If both husband and wife work, a common situation is that when he is ready to retire, she is not. Often she is younger (in second marriages, often considerably so), and she may have just gotten the wind in her sails. He may insist that she retire when she does not want to give up her work. Understandably, especially if she has returned to work after raising their children, her career might just be peaking. An ideal situation is when both want to retire at the same time. But in that case both husband and wife are losing their work, and they have to face each other twenty-four hours a day.

WORKING AFTER RETIREMENT

There are many reasons why you might want to continue to work after retirement. The most obvious one is the need for additional money. But many rewards of work, as we have discussed, go beyond the paycheck. Part-time work, for many, is the most painless transition into full-time retirement. Some taking early retirement might be young enough to want to consider a second career. Others might want to fulfill an old dream to start a business. For those who wish to continue doing paid work, the following are some options.

- *Part-time work* serves the purpose of earning extra income, and possibly also of getting out of the house and involved with people. A good vehicle for this are temp (temporary) jobs.

- *A second career* will take a little more effort and time and should be planned ahead. It is mainly for people who retire early enough to have the time to obtain more education or training for a new career.

- *Starting a business* is an option if you have skills or abilities that would lend themselves to starting a small business.

Temporary Jobs
A temporary job often fits neatly with retired people's needs. Although the majority of temp jobs are in the clerical field, there are

openings in a number of other categories. Now one can find well-qualified temps in medical practice or trying legal cases. No more just a way of securing a paycheck, temping can be a route to a permanent position and a way to stay in the labor market between full-time jobs.

Temps are hired and paid by the agency that assigns them to the job, not by the company for which they are doing the work. As any other employer would do, the temp agency handles the payroll, including withholdings of Social Security and premiums for unemployment insurance and workers compensation. In some cases the temp agency provides other benefits, such as health insurance, retirement plans, or paid sick leave. According to the National Association of Temporary Services (NATS), more than a million people work as temporary employees every day in the U.S. About 72 percent of these are women; one-third have college degrees.

Most people who turn to temp jobs do so because they cannot find steady jobs, and because it offers a possibility of leading to permanent employment. (This happens about 40 percent of the time, according to NATS.) Temping offers flexibility and the option to turn down a position if the job conditions don't suit you. You also escape the often exhaustive job search, which includes interviews with employers and uncertainties as to whether the job you accept is the right one for you. The temp agency screens the employer and the applicant and matches them to each other.

On the downside, temp jobs pay about 15 to 20 percent less than permanent employment, and there is no guarantee of steady employment. As a retiree you might be willing to pay that price for the freedom to set your own pace and choose your work schedule. Updating old skills and learning new ones will make you more in demand in the temp market and also probably bring higher pay. A temp agency's lack of health insurance and retirement plan may not be a concern for you if you are over sixty-five and covered by your own or your husband's Social Security and Medicare. Temp agencies are listed in your telephone directory. Some have staff members specializing in placing older people.

Other Part-Time Jobs

Should you want a full-time or part-time job on a regular basis, you will have to compete with younger job applicants. This in itself might prevent you from even trying. Clearly the field narrows as people pass into their sixties. If employers are so busy trying to get rid of current employees over fifty, why should they hire new ones? Well, they might. The reason for pushing older employees out of their jobs is not because they are old, but because they are expensive, having reached a pay level that is far above what their employer will have to pay for younger new employees in the same jobs. Older employees are also blocking the careers of younger ones, who might go looking elsewhere. If you are willing to settle for the pay of an entry-level job, or a position that is not on a career ladder, you might have a chance. Employers are also favorably disposed toward part-time employees because they don't have to pay them full benefits.

Older employees have a reputation for being responsible and reliable. You might also be considered a desirable employee in certain fields such as retirement homes, medical centers, schools, or as a receptionist, recreation director, or assistant. One seventy-year-old woman landed a full-time job as activities director at a large retirement apartment complex. At seventy-five, she is still employed and is loving it. She has no intention to stop working.

Starting a Business

Have you ever thought that you might possess a skill or some knowledge that could be parlayed into a viable small business? There are some legendary examples of large businesses starting small in garages or kitchens, in a storefront, or from a desk in a bedroom. Mrs.

Fields started her cookie empire in her kitchen. Hallmark was started by two brothers who sold postcards out of a shoe box. Older age should not limit your vision. Colonel Saunders started his Kentucky Fried Chicken business after his retirement. Leaving aside such astounding success stories, a small business can be something as simple as having a computer service, a baby-sitting service, a day-care center, or turning your accounting experience into a freelance job.

Self-employment offers some benefits, such as independence and the excitement of succeeding with something that is wholly your own. On the downside, small businesses have a notoriously high failure rate. You will probably need capital to get started, and you need some solid business knowledge. It is more often than not the business side of the small business that becomes the stumbling block.

The first step to take if you consider self-employment is to learn all the aspects of running a small business. The best source for information is the Small Business Administration (SBA), which usually maintains offices at Chambers of Commerce. They offer all the informational material you would need as well as workshops for beginners. If the SBA does not have an office in your community, you should write them. The SBA also sponsors SCORE (Service Corps of Retired Executives), a free consulting program for small-business owners and managers. Retired executives volunteer their time to counsel on issues from writing a business plan to marketing. Talk with someone you know who has experience running a small business. Also ask yourself the following questions:

- What do you have to offer? Assess the value of your skills, knowledge, or product. Is there a real lack of what you have to offer, or is your community saturated? Do you have the capital or tools needed to start?

- Would you be willing to learn and manage the business side of a business? Many people who start businesses have something worthwhile to market, but their lack of business experience presents difficulties. You need to know some accounting principles, be familiar with tax laws, be willing to spend time marketing your skill or product, and be willing to work sixteen hours a day to keep your business afloat.

❖ Do you have enough capital to keep the business going for a few years, until it shows a profit?

Volunteer Work

For many people volunteer work has proven to be the perfect activity in their postretirement years. There are countless choices as to kind of volunteer work, or where and when to work. Volunteering is more flexible than paid work, and at the same time it offers more structure than other leisure activities. Many have found that when the motivation of receiving money for work is removed, the intangible benefits can include the gift of good feelings, self-worth, and a sense of fulfillment from having made a contribution to the community or having helped individual people. Volunteer work for many might hold that elusive meaning that is sometimes lacking in older people's lives.

Volunteering tends to be equated with service, helping behavior, and altruism. The reward is often enriched feelings of optimism and self-esteem.

In the past, volunteering was seen as especially suited to women's natural inclination to serve and play supportive roles in society and in their homes. It was an integral part of women's societal role. Women's-movement advocates saw the ideology of volunteerism as a deterrent to the liberation of women into an equal status with men and attempted to redefine volunteerism. Service volunteering, they said, is no more natural to women than to men. Women's advocates argued that we need to focus on our economic survival and this should include change-oriented volunteering—removing the barriers to our equality through political action. Thus volunteering includes interest group activities as well as service volunteering, all of which are equally valuable to individuals and to a healthy society.

If you are planning to make volunteering a serious activity in your life, it is worthwhile to make a step-by-step plan for finding the type of volunteer job that will be satisfying to you. This plan is essentially the same as one a career-planning expert would recommend to a person trying to find a job and establish a career. Many people have done volunteer work during their working years or while raising a family, and need little instruction in how to find the right volunteer job. But for some of you who might have little experience with and knowledge about the volunteer world, here is some general advice:

Clarify your motives for volunteering. What do you want to get out of your volunteer activities? Do you have a special interest that you want to support? Do you have a skill that you want to use or develop? Do you have a strong need to be helpful, to give service? Do you need social contacts and group belongingness? Do you want to develop a skill and further your growth? Do you want something that helps structure your life? Do you want a purpose and a goal? Do you like to work with a project? Do you have a cause that you want to further?

Clarify what kind of work you would like to do, the environment you like to work in, and the people you like to work with. Do you want autonomy or do you prefer working in a group? What are you good at doing? Do you want to be in charge or do you prefer to take orders?

Be willing to be trained (for example, as a museum docent). Thus armed with self-knowledge and a good idea of what kind of volunteer work is available in your community, you can set out to find your perfect spot. You are sure to be welcome in many places. Thousands of service organizations would come to a halt if they could not find volunteers. Many good causes would never get off the ground without a devout cadre of motivated people. Moreover, a person with the forethought and initiative to do the research you have been doing will be a valuable asset wherever she chooses to work.

Research what is available in your community. Volunteering takes place in all sectors of society, in nonprofit organizations, in the corporate world, and in state and local government agencies. You might start at the volunteer bureau in your community or go directly to the place where you are considering working. Volunteer groups in large organizations and agencies are usually headed by a volunteer director or overseen by the personnel department. Request interviews with them and bring a list of questions:

- What kind of work will you do?

- What skills are required?

- Who will you work with?

- How will you be supervised?

- What are the requirements concerning hours, scheduling, and so on?

- Does the organization offer skills training?

- Is there any compensation (such as transportation, lunch, or watching the opera or theater production you are ushering)?

- What are the future prospects? Are there provisions to enable volunteers to move up or to other positions in the organization?

Remember, you are the one who is doing the interviewing, not the other way around.

In spite of the often-voiced assertion that volunteer work is gratifying because it involves helping others, people frequently donate their labor to causes that are close to their hearts or that will benefit themselves, family members, or groups they belong to. For example, mothers volunteer in their children's schools, working people volunteer in trade or professional organizations. Families often support an association that fights an illness someone in their family has. Many work in fund-raising efforts for schools, churches, or associations that lend social status to themselves and their families.

As an older woman, you might want to find an organization that either serves older people or that works to further the cause of older women. There are a number of programs designed especially for retirees, and many services to older people are performed by retirees. The federal government's Grandparents Program is one such program.

If you want to play a more active role or become an advocate for older women, you should join the Older Women's League or the AARP. Environmental advocacy organizations and political organizations are chronically short of volunteers and would welcome you with open arms.

Veteran volunteers are often high-activity people, who have always done many things, such as been involved in church, community, recreational, and family activities. They tend to be extroverted, outgoing people who are energized by contact with others. Such people usually do not have problems finding activities in retirement.

It is the person who has never volunteered who might find it awkward searching for a suitable volunteer task. If you are such a person, you might "volunteer" on an informal basis by helping neighbors and friends or taking care of family members, grandchildren, or aged parents. This type of volunteering often goes unmentioned; it is an invisible activity but is nevertheless of great personal and social importance. And it answers your need for community and meaningful activities.

Whatever kind of volunteering you choose, several payoffs may accrue as unintended side effects. Volunteering might solve your recreational needs, such as ushering at the opera or theater. It can provide personal growth as you learn new skills and master new tasks. It might provide an avenue to a new career or even lead to a paying job.

LIFELONG LEARNING

No other area is as rich in opportunities and promises for growth, excitement, and meaning for older people as learning and education. For those now retired, education was seen as a young person's opportunity to acquire occupational or professional skills and competence. This is no longer true. Learning is now seen as a lifelong process, and education is something that many will turn to in midlife or later.

The benefits of learning and education for older people are many. Continued learning has been demonstrated to have a positive effect on maintaining intellectual functioning into old age. Learning also helps increase self-esteem and affords a feeling of achievement. Signing up for courses or seminars and keeping a schedule for attendance and study is one way to structure your time, another important aspect of postretirement life. As a bonus you will meet people, exchanging views and information, developing new friendships with some. In a learning mode you will look at the world with more curiosity and interest—a crucial attitude for finding meaning in your life.

Education does not have to be formal or structured. There are an abundance of different ways to learn. Depending on what retirement phase you are in, what your financial needs are, and what kind of activities you value and enjoy, you will have different motivations for pursuing learning activities.

Studies for a Second Career

If you wish to pursue a second career it might be necessary to get additional education. Before committing to a lengthy degree or certification program you would do well to enlist the services of a career planning expert. Inquire at your nearest community college about career development programs such as classes, workshops, seminars, or individual counseling. They have the tools for testing and values clarification that could help you make decisions about a second career.

Depending on the area you pursue, you might need a certificate or degree, for example in gerontology. Maybe you would like to go back to an interrupted career, such as teaching, and will need accreditation. If starting a business is your goal, no degree is necessary, but you might benefit from taking courses in business-related subjects, such as accounting, contracts, or marketing, or to learn more about the business you are considering.

There are ways to fashion viable second careers if you're willing to learn some of the in's and out's. For example, you might offer consultation services in an area where you have expertise, or you could acquire computer skills in word processing or accounting.

Useful Knowledge
Pastimes such as maintaining our homes and enjoying our hobbies will be easier if we learn the best way to do them. For instance, do you like to refinish furniture? Do you want to reupholster your sofa? Is the wallpaper in your bathroom in need of replacement? Have you harbored a desire to learn how to weave? Do you want to learn the basics of a foreign language so you can communicate with the locals when traveling to a foreign country? What about learning money management skills? Do you want to better understand health and nutrition for older people? There is likely to be a course for almost anything you wish to learn.

Fun and Pleasure
Certain learning experiences are stimulating and open our minds to new vistas and perspectives of life and the world. Courses in the arts, literature, music, or any number of humanities programs afford per-

sonal growth. You might work for a degree in something just for the fun of it, or take specific classes that interest you. These opportunities will broaden your outlook on life, possibly satisfying a thirst for understanding and awareness that you could not respond to during your working years. Hobby courses provide useful knowledge that overlaps with pleasure. Learning is often fun, and many find it a pleasurable activity in itself.

Learning Opportunities

Instruction in an array of subjects is offered in various educational settings, and much of it is free or discounted for seniors. You will find courses on just about everything in universities, community colleges, trade schools, museums, senior centers, and libraries. These are often listed under Adult Education in course catalogs.

Many community colleges offer courses for credit over public television channels. For those of you with access to a computer, there are many educational programs available on disks, and the Internet is a vast source of information.

Thanks to legislation enacted during the sixties and seventies, there is support for a wide variety of programs for older adults. In most states, universities and colleges have policies that waive tuition for people over sixty or sixty-five. Such tuition waivers sometimes depend on space availability in classes or may limit participation to auditing classes (taking courses without earning credit). Some programs are specifically designed for seniors.

Other sources include craft stores, which will furnish information about arts and crafts courses and presentations. Health organizations such as hospitals often hold conferences and consultations with training. Some organizations present interesting speakers on various subjects at their meetings. Libraries, continuing education programs, senior centers, and museums are also worth looking into. Some bookstores feature readings by published authors. Finally, inquire into what the AARP might offer in your community.

Outside of the classroom, Elderhostel and Interhostel are popular ways to travel and meet people while learning.

Barriers to Learning

An older person might have several barriers to overcome before taking advantage of educational opportunities. Some barriers are psychological. You might feel that you are too old, that education is for younger people. If your earlier education was limited, you might have hesitations about your ability to keep up with the requirements of a college course and be afraid of feeling out of place in an academic environment. You might feel it pretentious to take time to learn something that does not have a practical application, such as arts or humanities. That is, you might suffer from an "It's not for me" attitude.

Other barriers are of a practical kind. You might have difficulties with transportation or with the cost of the courses you want. If you have physical problems such as hearing loss or eye problems, it may be difficult to find the information you need. If you live too far away from an educational institution to attend classes regularly, you might investigate opportunities for education by correspondence. Many cities have TV channels that offer college courses. A library in your community will be able to help you.

A third kind of barrier is the sometimes intractable nature of educational institutions. Requirements for enrollment, inflexible deadlines, and rigid bureaucratic rules might be more than you want to cope with. Before you give up, find out if your nearest college has special programs for seniors that might have more flexible requirements.

LEISURE AND RECREATION

Hobbies, travel, cultural events, and socializing often become the mainstay of activities in later life. While some of this has a price tag, many events and activities are available at little or no cost. Wherever you live, the best place to start is probably your local library, which will have listings of freebies in your area. There might be groups to join, such as hiking clubs, folk dance groups, or reading clubs. Museums often have a free day each month, and there are often free concerts in schools and churches. Senior centers usually offer many free activities, such as exercise classes, speakers, and discussion groups. They might also have recreation rooms for pool, TV watching, and socializing as well as a lunch room. The great outdoors is, of course, always available for fishing, hiking, swimming, and camping.

DON'T POSTPONE—LIVE NOW

You cannot expect that the activities that suit you at age sixty will answer your needs for the rest of your life. Over the twenty to thirty years of retirement your circumstances and interests will change, and you may go through phases of diminished strength and ability that don't allow you to carry out strenuous activities. It's important not to postpone the plans that depend on health and vigor. Learn to ski now, take the mountain climbing tour as soon as you can, join a folk dancing group without delay, don't put off a regular exercise program. If you want to travel, consider doing it this year. All this activity will help build up your vigor for your later years. Plan for yourself now, expecting that in the later years, when most people slow down physically, you can then choose activities that keep you closer to home. Your life can be made as full and rewarding as you wish. It is up to each of us to take action and decide how to shape our lives as older women.

Chapter Six

CAREGIVING:
A Woman's Issue

For women, caregiving is an expected duty; for men, it is an unexpected expression of compassion.
—Tish Sommers and Laurie Shields

CARING FOR OTHERS HAS been an integral part of who we are as women. Women have been the primary caregivers for their children, as well as other family members, throughout society. Even though women's place in society and the work world has changed, caring for a sick and aging spouse, sibling, or partner is still seen as primarily a woman's responsibility.

Approximately three-fourths of all caregivers for older disabled family members are women, according to the AARP Women's Initiative. Most older women can anticipate being in a caregiving role as they age. Yet many women are not conscious of this expectation until something happens, and they are thrown into the position of giving care totally unprepared.

While many chronic illnesses of later life, such as Alzheimer's disease and arthritis, progress slowly, an acute illness such as heart attack or stroke demands immediate care. At first, our assistance may be needed for only a few hours per week. As the situation changes, we may gradually find ourselves taking on more and more care responsibilities. At some point, either overnight or over a long time, we become full-time caregivers. Because women tend to outlive men, and often marry older men, they may become caregivers to their husband while at the same time caring for an aging parent.

Although being a caregiver can be rewarding, the lack of support by our communities and the lack of a national health system that assists caregivers make caregiving an act of love fraught with many consequences. Even if a woman is healthy, the physical and emotional demands of long-term care on her life are profound. Many caregivers suffer from medical problems that develop from years of physical strain engendered by long-term care of another person. Some suffer from back problems developed from lifting another person. Others develop stomachaches, headaches, and other illnesses. Many become depressed.

In the past, women could expect family assistance with their caregiving tasks, traditionally from daughters and daughters-in-law, but this has changed. Younger women are no longer readily available for this role, because most work outside the home; many are single parents and lack the time and resources. Many families live far apart and are therefore unable to give hands-on help. It therefore becomes all the more important for older women to know how to access community resources and to plan ahead for the time when the major responsibility for care of another may be theirs.

Although caregiving is a very trying experience, there are positive aspects. It may lead to feelings of satisfaction in our own competence and ability. Caring for another may lead to a deeper, more fulfilling relationship with that person. However, it can also result in grave physical, mental, and financial consequences. How we are able to handle our particular caregiving circumstance will depend on our health, what finances we have available to us, our housing, our age, and what family assistance we can call on. Whatever our feelings or circumstances, full-time caregiving changes our life. The fundamental problem we face is how to do our best in balancing our obligations and commitments to others and to ourselves.

The goal of this chapter is to clarify the issues involved and to offer information, resources, and encouragement. Many of us will be caregivers at a time when we might well be least able to tackle the job. By being prepared for problems, recognizing our limitations, learning what assistance is available, and having a plan, we will be better able to handle the task. However, situations vary, and what works for one family may not work for another.

In order to decide how to handle your situation, you should first identify what your problems are now and what help you need. Later you can reassess your needs as the situation changes.

Assessing Your Caregiving Situation

Although your caregiving chores may gradually increase over a number of years, most people become caregivers without warning. Most long-term care is done at home, rather than in an institution. A wife usually wants to keep a loved one in familiar surroundings, or she feels caring for the person is her responsibility. Sometimes this is the only option, when nursing homes and other out-of-home care is simply too expensive.

The first step in managing caregiving is to assess what needs to be done, what you are able to do, and what assistance you need.

As you appraise the situation, look at the whole picture—the person you are caring for, yourself, and other available assistance, both practical and emotional. Recognize your responsibilities, but also your limitations. Know what you are capable of, and do not take on more than you can handle. Acknowledge your own feelings about the situation. You may feel guilty, helpless, frustrated, or afraid of the loss of the one you are caring for. These feelings are not unusual for the situation and are felt by most caregivers. The following questions will help you determine your needs and options.

What is the "patient's" condition? What is the prognosis? Many caregivers state that they can handle short-term care of someone who is expected to recuperate quickly, such as after an operation.

What level of care is needed? There are times when the care needed may be more than you can physically deal with. This is the time when you should consider bringing additional services into your home, or perhaps other alternatives, such as alternative housing. If this is not possible you may have to consider nursing home placement.

What level of care can you provide? Your health must be taken into consideration when trying to realistically ascertain what amount of care you will be able to offer. The actual physical labor involved in caregiving places a great deal of stress on the body. Frequently, heavy lifting is involved. The one being cared for may need help in and out of bed and getting to the toilet or shower. The bed may need to be changed, and there will be extra laundry if the person is incontinent. Many older caregivers suffer from degenerative diseases such as arthritis, which will be made worse with heavy lifting, and so on. In fact, the majority of people sixty-five and over do have at least one chronic physical condition. You cannot ignore your own physical problems or you may reach the point when you will no longer be able to offer any care.

What assistance do you need now? What might you need later? Many elders have limited incomes; since assistance can be expensive it is important to consider these two questions together. In fact, lack of finances or fear of impoverishment leads many older caregivers to decide not to purchase such services. If you know what to expect in the future it will be easier to decide what services you can afford now. Be sure to check what services are available without cost.

What services are available? Where can you look for help? First find out what help your family, friends, and neighbors can offer. The section in this chapter on services and resources should help you access the services that you need or can afford.

This is the time to be realistic about your needs and to consider every possible alternative. Sometimes there are options that you would not think of yourself, such as a hospital bed with a trapeze bar that can allow a person to lift him- or herself out of bed. This will solve a major problem. Other assistive devices such as bath chairs, nonskid mats, and grab bars facilitate independent bathing and toileting. Supports, such as walkers, prevent falls. Seek help with the assessment process from your physician, your pastor, a social service agency, or friends and relatives who might be able to suggest other useful alternatives. Perhaps your care recipient may be capable of helping with his or her own care. Offer only the amount of care needed at the time. Save your energy for when it will be needed most.

Share decision making with the one you are caring for and other family members, if possible. Only make decisions for the care receiver if he or she is incapable of making them. Once you have completed your assessment it is time to make a plan. Remember, situations change, and therefore plans may change, but a workable plan now may prevent an overwhelming sense of hopelessness.

MAKING A CAREGIVING PLAN

Making a plan of care will involve the following:

* understanding the one you are caring for and involving the person in the decision-making process

* knowing your own health and what it will allow you to do

* knowing financial and legal issues involved

* knowing available services and resources

+ beginning your plan of action

Understand the One You Care For

The person being cared for will have many feelings about their illness, including fears of helplessness, pain, or death. Many have feelings of embarrassment over losing control of their body functions. Others fear being a burden on the family.

Open communication helps in understanding the other person's feelings and fears. It is a challenge to accept help without feeling a loss of independence. Remember that feelings, attitudes, and behavior are often distorted by the illness or medications being used to treat it. Simply using good listening skills and accepting a person's feelings without necessarily approving of them is invaluable. Maximize the independence of the persons being cared for. Do not undermine the person's capabilities. Provide information so he or she can make as many of their own decisions as possible.

Although the caregiver must set limits on what she can live with, understanding what is being expressed and being willing to compromise is essential to retaining the autonomy of both people involved.

Consider Your Own Health and What You Are Able to Do

Don't try to handle all caregiving duties by yourself. You are not a failure if you ask for help. If you already have physical problems, the added burden of caregiving could increase your problem and make you unable to give any care. It is unrealistic to think that you can do everything by yourself. Seek all the assistance you can get for this difficult time in your life. It is important to understand that this is a time to ask for whatever assistance you can get and that you have not failed even if you eventually have to place the one you are caring for in a nursing home. Half of all nursing home admissions are due to caregiver burnout.

Pay attention to your feelings and share them with your pastor, friends, and family. Find time to relax and do things for yourself such as reading a book, gardening, or writing a letter.

Set limits on the amount and kind of care you can give, and never give more help than is needed.

Be Aware of Legal and Financial Issues of Caregiving

In order to plan, you must know what financial resources are available to you and what legal documents may be needed. You will also need to know how to access needed funds. If you are a caregiving spouse you may already be handling the finances. Even so, the following information may help in planning for the future. If you are caring for someone other than your spouse, the following may help you understand your alternatives.

As you consider the following legal and financial information, it is important to remember that the person you are caring for may have difficulty relinquishing control of his or her finances. Being ill does not mean a person wants to give up his or her autonomy. Taking away a person's control over finances is a serious matter. Take only the actions that must be taken, but also be sure that you have the information you may need in the future to manage your care recipient's affairs. Consider what legal instruments might be best for your situation and be sure to seek legal advice. Your goal should be to give as much assistance as needed without usurping control.

When considering your financial situation, investigate any entitlement programs that might be available. Free services will help you augment the funds needed for care. Start by checking with your physician to see if the person you are caring for is entitled to any in-home care paid for by Medicare. Although Medicare does not normally cover long-term nursing home or home-health care, you should still confer with your recipient's physician regarding any health problem your care recipient has that would give him or her entitlement to these services. Medicare covers certain health needs, but not all physicians are knowledgeable about the rules. If your physician is not knowledgeable about Medicare coverage, call your local Visiting Nurses Association to do an assessment of your care recipient. Ask if they charge for this service or if the assessment is free. If they determine that the person you are caring for is entitled to services under Medicare, they will handle the paperwork and develop a plan of care with your physician. If the person you are caring for belongs to an HMO, investigate what assistance it can provide.

Next, you should check insurance coverage to ascertain whether the one you are caring for has any long-term health insurance coverage, perhaps through a former employer.

Medicaid and Supplemental Security Income (programs for those with limited income) are entitlements that might be available for nursing home care or in-home care. Availability will differ according to where you live. Call your county social service department to check on this. They will do an assessment and inform you of what services are available.

Another way to increase your available assets is by taking out a reverse mortgage on your home. A reverse mortgage will enable you to transform your home equity into a monthly income while you remain in your home. (See chapter four for more information on this program.)

The Veterans Administration (VA) will provide or pay for home-care services for veterans who have service-connected disabilities or as follow-up to care provided in a VA hospital. The in-home services provided will depend on the veterans' status and whether the disability is service-connected. Eligibility requirements can be complex. Contact your local VA office for further information on what is available and how and where to apply.

In order to pay for needed services you will have to know how to access your care recipient's funds when necessary. The following information will explain ways to do this. You should, however, consult an attorney for more information.

Joint bank accounts may be an easy way to pay your care recipient's bills. A joint account can be set up by either putting your name on an account as an "additional authorized signature" or "joint ownership with a right of survivorship." Right of survivorship means that when one owner of the account dies, the account belongs to the survivor.

A joint account requires trust on the part of both parties. Some states permit creditors of the helping relative to access some of the person's funds in a joint account. If not properly handled, a joint account can present complications in terms of taxes and eligibility for Medicaid and SSI. To avoid such complications, a caregiving relative (other than the spouse) should not deposit any of her money into the account or withdraw money for personal use.

A *power of attorney* is a written document that gives one person legal authority to act on another person's behalf in financial transactions. It can be useful for someone who is capable of directing his or her finances but needs assistance in conducting personal business. The individual does not lose the right to manage his or her finances, but extends that right to an additional person.

Having trust in the person to whom a power of attorney is given is crucial. No one supervises the person who has a power of attorney (except the care recipient), and abuses are possible. The person given a power of attorney has only those powers specified in the document, so the power can be limited to explicit purposes. The power of attorney must be in writing, signed and notarized. Although standard forms are available in bookstores, it is best to get help from an attorney. Call Legal Assistance for Seniors for help and advice. You might also inquire whether they have a notary available to come to your home to notarize the document.

The person authorizing a power of attorney can revoke it at any time. When revoking a power of attorney, the revocation must be recorded in the county where property is located.

A power of attorney may end if the one you are caring for becomes mentally incapacitated and loses his or her decision-making ability. It also terminates upon a person's death, or upon an expiration date specified in the power of attorney. Some financial institutions only recognize a power of attorney drawn up on their forms; therefore, it may be necessary to complete their individual forms.

A durable power of attorney differs from the above power of attorney in that it does not terminate if the person granting the power becomes mentally incapacitated. It can be written such that it goes into effect only if and when a person becomes incapacitated or incompetent. However, it is sometimes hard to recognize when this has happened, and the holder of the power of attorney may have difficulty getting the power honored by banks and other institutions.

The durable power of attorney, therefore, avoids conservatorship/guardianship proceedings in the event of incapacity. In most states, medical and health care can also be determined by a durable power of attorney.

A durable power of attorney should be drawn up by an attorney. State laws regarding this document vary; therefore, if you are out of state (a long-distance caregiver) it is important that the attorney you choose is licensed in the state in which the care recipient lives. In many states, all powers of attorney are presumed to be durable unless limited in their wording.

A living trust is one way a person can assure management and protection of assets if he or she becomes incapacitated. A trust is a three-party arrangement that transfers designated assets from one person (the grantor) to another person (the trustee), who holds and manages the assets for the benefit of the third person (the beneficiary). The grantor, trustee, and beneficiary may be the same person. The trust agreement contains specific instructions about the management and distribution of the assets to the beneficiary.

There are two types of living trusts: revocable and irrevocable. A revocable trust remains in a person's control during his or her life-time, then passes to the beneficiary upon the person's death. The person whose trust it is (the grantor) can revoke the trust at his or her discretion. Changes to the trust can also be made at any time at the discretion of the grantor. An irrevocable trust is controlled by the trustee. The grantor loses control of the assets.

Assets in a living trust avoid probate. (There can be tax consequences, however, depending on the amount of the assets.) Although forms for setting up living trusts can be purchased at stationary stores, a lawyer should be consulted in setting up a trust. It is particularly important that the person drafting the living trust is knowledgeable about restrictions on Medicaid eligibility for beneficiaries of living trusts in case the grantor may need long-term care.

A *will* is a way for someone to leave property to persons or charities that he or she wishes to inherit it. For an explanation of wills and why they should be considered, see chapter three.

A representative payee, such as yourself, may be needed if the person you are caring for is unable to manage his or her Social Security, veteran's pension, Railroad Retirement, or public benefits checks. This device is useful when your care-recipient's expenses can be covered by a benefit check. The representative payee is not empowered to gain access to the person's savings accounts or other assets. (If you are the spouse, or if lack of trust is not an issue, direct deposit into a joint checking account might work better.)

To arrange to become your care recipient's representative payee, contact the appropriate agency (such as Social Security or Veterans Affairs) for an application form and instructions on how to file. Medical confirmation that your care recipient is not able to manage benefit payments will be required. Notice will be sent to your care recipient, who can consent or object to your being named representative payee. If you become a representative payee, you will be given information on how funds are to be held, managed, and disbursed, as well as any accounting that will be required.

Conservatorship is a court process that secures an individual's right to manage another person's financial affairs when that person becomes unable to do so. It can be created only through the legal system. An attorney must file a petition for you with the court, and a judge will decide if your care recipient is competent to manage his or her affairs or if a conservator should be appointed. In many states, a hearing is held only if someone objects in writing to the court.

A family member may serve as a conservator. For a large or complex estate, an attorney may be appointed. When no one else is available, a public guardian may be appointed as conservator. Once a conservator is appointed, your care receiver will lose the right to make his or her own financial decisions. Other rights, however, remain intact unless a guardian is appointed.

The conservator is responsible to the court and must make an annual accounting. Most states require the conservator to purchase a bond equal to the value of the estate they are overseeing. There are expenses associated with a conservatorship, such as a filing fee, legal fees, bonds, and accounting fees. The conservator might receive a fee that will be set by the court. The conservator may also be reimbursed for expenses incurred managing the estate and for the accounting costs. A conservator may be removed and replaced by the court that appointed the conservator.

If you suspect your care recipient may not be able to manage his or her personal finances, it is prudent to consider what legal and financial instruments will be needed, then discuss it with an attorney to determine the wisest course of action.

After you obtain any needed legal documents and know what financial resources are available for your use, you can determine which of the services described below are possible to assist you with your caregiving.

Find Services and Resources for Caregiving

The following section will help you learn what resources are available, their cost, and where to locate them. Some resources will be free, others are not. Your financial situation will determine whether you will have to rely on family and friends for assistance or if you will be able to hire outside professional help.

Most communities have some or all of the following services. Whether you live in an urban or rural area will make a difference in the range and types of services available. The types of services to look for and consider are:

* information and referral services

* home health care

* respite services

* miscellaneous services and resources

Information and referral services are available to you even if there are no referral agencies in your local area. (See Resources.)

* *Eldercare Locator.* This organization is a nationwide directory assistance service to help older people and caregivers locate local support resources for aging Americans. The service is free.

* *Department of Aging.* For information and referral on senior services in your area, contact your local Department of Aging. This should be listed under government services in your telephone directory. It may be listed as the Area Agency on Aging or state Department of Aging.

* *Discharge planner.* If your care recipient is in the hospital, you are entitled to the services of a discharge planner. They are usually nurses or social workers who provide advice on nursing care, special medical equipment, community resources, out-of-home

placement, and so on. This service should be free and should be sought in preparation for discharge.

- *Medical social worker.* They are social workers who help the care recipient and family cope with illness. They usually can assist with locating community resources including benefit programs and planning for alternate care, such as day care. Contact your local hospital or Visiting Nurses Association for more information.

- *Care manager (care coordinator).* If you need help locating and arranging for assistance in caring for your recipient, you might consider hiring a care manager to assist you. A care manager can coordinate the different kinds of services that may be needed and can sometimes help sort out financial questions. Care managers usually charge between $50 and $75 per hour. The National Association of Geriatric Case Managers offers free referrals and publishes a directory.

Home health care services. Many times they are the enabling service that prevents institutionalization. Your care recipient's needs will determine which of the following services will be helpful.

- *Home care nurse.* These nurses provide skilled care for patients with acute (recent onset) or long-term (chronic) illness. Call your local Visiting Nurses Association or nurses registry.

- *Home health agencies.* These agencies are licensed by the state to provide nursing and related services in the home. Home health services may include skilled nursing, social work services, physical therapy, occupational therapy, speech therapy, and home health support. Home health aides, supervised by registered nurses, assist clients with activities of daily living, such as feeding, bathing, dressing, and ambulation. Some agencies have lists of both Medicare-certified and noncertified providers. Contact the

Visiting Nurses Association in your area for more information.

- *Hospice.* When a physician certifies that a Medicare beneficiary is terminally ill, that beneficiary may choose to receive hospice care provided by a Medicare-certified agency. Hospices offer comprehensive programs of care including nursing, pain control, medical counseling, caregiver respite, and other social services to help the patient and family cope with dying. Although there are some facility-based hospices, most programs are home based. When a hospice is chosen for your care-recipient, Medicare will cover most of the cost.

To locate a hospice service, contact your local hospital, Visiting Nurses Association, cancer society, the National Hospice Association, or your telephone directory.

- *Nurse's aides.* Trained for care in the home, these aides can help when licensed nurses are not required. Call your nurse's aide registry for referrals.

- *Occupational therapists.* Many patients with long-term disabilities can develop adaptive techniques. These therapists assist in teaching such techniques. Call your local hospital for referrals.

- *Physical therapists.* These therapists teach patients and families rehabilitation techniques to improve strength, endurance, and ambulation. Call your local hospital for referrals.

Respite services. These may be the single most important services caregivers need. Their purpose is to offer temporary relief from the daily responsibility of primary caregiving. These services are available from hospice programs, and you should also seek this type of help from friends, neighbors, and relatives. Some churches can also provide respite.

- *Adult day-care and health centers.* These offer social, recreational, and therapeutic activities for older people. If your care recipient is well enough to use this service, it would be a time of respite for you as caregiver. Check your phone book or Department of Aging for more information. These services may be offered free for those with limited incomes; costs to others vary. Many long-term care insurance policies cover these services, which can run $50 a day and up. Check to see if the facility you are considering has sliding-scale fees.

- *Nursing and board and care homes for respite.* Another alternative respite program involves the use of a nursing home or other caregiving facility while you take a vacation. To locate such a long-term respite program, contact your local Area Agency on Aging, a local senior center, or call local nursing or board and care homes.

Miscellaneous services and resources. The following are some of the other useful services or resources that may be available in your area.

- *American Red Cross.* This organization lends medical equipment, such as wheelchairs, crutches, and walkers. They may also have vans to take frail or ill people to medical appointments. Call your local chapter for more information.

- *American Cancer Society.* The American Cancer Society lends medical equipment in some areas. They sometimes take frail or ill people to medical appointments. Call your local chapter for more information.

- *Homemaker service agencies.* These agencies are not necessarily certified. They can provide workers to help with light housekeeping, meal preparation, personal care, shopping, laundry, and so on. Check your phone book for these services. Senior centers and the Department of Aging's information and referral unit usually keep names of persons (unscreened) who are interested in homemaker, home health aide, or companion positions. The local office of the state's Employment Development Department is also a source of help in locating domestic workers. Sometimes neighbors and friends who have been assisted are the best source of this information.

- *Meals on Wheels.* This program, which is funded under the Department of Aging, delivers hot meals to homebound elders who are unable to cook. The program may charge fees on a sliding scale. Call your local senior center or Department of Aging to locate this service.

- *Support groups.* A support group can be a valuable source of comfort as well as a great place to share information on community resources. Many caregivers find that sharing their experiences and feelings helps relieve stress and lets them cope more effectively. To locate a caregivers support group call your Department of Aging, a mental health clinic, hospice, or a hospital. If such a group is not available, consider starting your own.

- *Other sources of information.* Your local senior center may have a staff person who can make referrals. Family service agencies often offer case management or referral services. Your local library may have a list of resources.

Once you determine what services you need and what resources are available, it is time to make your care plan. The Home Care Plans chart at the end of this chapter can guide you. It is not conclusive and will not fit all situations, but it will help you prioritize how to proceed.

The following are some of the tasks that may be needed at times during your caregiving: bathing, dressing, and toileting your care-recipient, as well as cooking, cleaning, doing laundry, handling finances, giving shots and other medications, and changing bandages and intravenous tubes. You will probably also need to do such chores as shopping and making visits to the physician's office. If you cannot afford to hire assistance with these tasks, and help through Medicaid is not available, it may be necessary to enlist the help of family members and friends.

Begin Your Plan of Action

Discuss the planning with the one you are caring for to determine what assistance they can provide toward their own care. Make a realistic list of the type of help you need, such as nursing assistance, Meals on Wheels, transportation, and so on. Use the services and resource list above for suggestions.

- Assess your housing arrangements. Can you modify your home to make it caregiving-friendly? Would alternative housing be better?

- Contact information and referral organizations to learn what services are available. Then get in touch with any suggested free services. If the person you are caring for is on Medicaid, call the Department of Welfare or social services agency to ascertain whether any services are available to you.

- If you desire and funds permit, now is the time to contact a care manager who can help with your plan and can locate and hire services for you.

- Share your list of needs with friends, neighbors, and relatives to see who can offer assistance. Many times neighbors will pick up groceries for you when they do their shopping. One of your children may be able to take over the paperwork, such as submitting medical bills. Someone else may make calls for you to locate the services you need.

- Make a plan for respite care. If you plan time for yourself away from your caregiving, you will be less likely to be overwhelmed.

Part of this respite time might be used to join a support group. Being with others who understand what you are going through, who will listen and support you, can be very healing.

◆ In order to have more time for yourself, consider ordering Meals on Wheels and hiring a homemaker or home health aide to help with chores or personal care.

HIRING IN-HOME SUPPORT SERVICES

If you are planning to hire outside help, be sure that you have liability insurance to cover an employee who may be injured while working for you. Ask any home health agency you are considering using whether they insure their workers.

Before looking for paid in-home help, make a list of the services you will want performed. Since prices and services vary, you should contact several sources, such as friends, agencies, or a care manager. If you use an agency, rather than doing the hiring yourself, you may have to pay more but you will avoid having to advertise, interview, and check references.

If you hire an employee directly, rather than from an agency, you are required by law to withhold Social Security taxes from his or her paychecks and make payments to the Internal Revenue Service. If, however, the person you are hiring works as an independent contractor, he or she will pay their own Social Security.

Write a job description and contract that includes the duties to be performed, salary, hours of work, and so on. (A sample contract is located at the end of this chapter.) Having such an agreement is essential to avoid disputes. Be as specific as possible in the contract to lessen any chance of a disagreement. If the job involves special skills such as lifting your care recipient into the bathtub or giving medications, the worker should be trained and experienced in those skills.

Interviewing a Prospective Employee

You do not need to interview every person who applies. First ask them if they have done this kind of work before and if they can supply references. Personally interview those who you feel may fulfill your requirements.

You might want to ask a friend or relative to sit in on the interview. If at all possible, your care recipient should be present.

Have a copy of your sample contract ready for the applicant to read. You can use some of the suggested questions below; other questions may come to mind as you interview.

- Where have you worked before? What kind of duties did you perform? How long did you work there?

- How do you feel about caring for an elderly or disabled person?

- Have you done similar kinds of work?

- What is your attitude about smoking, drinking, or using drugs?

- Do you have any emotional or physical problems that might hinder you in the job?

- How do you handle a person who is angry, depressed, or confused?

- Will you be able to discuss with me issues that create problems for you?

- How long are you willing to stay on this job?

- How much advance notice can you give if you are unable to work?

- Are you licensed to drive? Do you have a car?

Ask for several work-related references and a personal one. Explain to the applicants that you will need to check their references before making a decision. Never hire anyone without checking references! Set a time when you will get back to the prospective employee.

Questions to Ask a Prospective Agency

If you decide to hire through a home health agency, check the Better Business Bureau to see whether any complaints have been lodged against the agency. The following questions will help you interview a prospective agency.

- Do you pay the payroll tax for your in-home support person?

- Is the person trained to perform required duties?

- How long has this person worked for your agency?

- Does the prospective employee have references?

- How much do you charge per hour?

- How much do you pay the employee per hour?

- Do I have to employ the person a minimum number of hours per week or month?

- Are your employees bonded?

- Do you carry liability insurance for your employees?

- Do you provide backup help if the person is unable to work?

- Will Medicare or Medicaid cover the services of this employee?

- Does the employee have transportation?

- Is the employee licensed to drive?

- Is the employee supervised by your agency?

- How do I terminate the employee's services?

After you have checked references and chosen your in-home employee, keep communication open between you. Give praise when earned and make time to discuss and resolve any problems that may arise. To avoid problems always ask your employee for receipts if they do any purchasing for you; put your valuables away to avoid temptation.

If you hire your employee from an agency, keep in touch with the agency. If you are dissatisfied tell them why and what can be done to remedy the situation.

If your first employee is not satisfactory, do not get discouraged. Take time to figure out what went wrong and try again.

No matter how hard you try and how many services you are able to bring into your home, the possibility may arise that you can no longer continue as caregiver. After investigating other alternatives such as board and care facilities, you may find that a nursing home is the necessary solution. If this should happen you will need to know how to choose and pay for a nursing home.

CHOOSING AND FINANCING A NURSING HOME

Once you decide that nursing home care is needed, you may feel overwhelmed. It is normal to feel anxious, angry, guilty, depressed, or scared at the thought of making such a decision as well as feeling relieved that you will no longer have the major care role. Selecting a nursing home is one of the most important and difficult decisions you and your care recipient will have to make.

Planning ahead is one of the best ways to ease the stress that accompanies the transition; you will be more assured that you have chosen a good facility that meets your needs. Ideally, you would have ample time to consider your options, but usually the need for a nursing home happens quickly.

The task of finding the right kind of home and the services you desire is a time-consuming effort. Finding the right facility is important, because this may be your care recipient's home for the rest of his or her life. If you can, involve him or her in the decision-making process as much as possible. When people enter nursing homes, they don't lose their basic human rights or need for respect, encouragement, friendship, and love. They need to retain as much control over the events in their daily lives as possible. You will both be more accepting of the decision if you cooperate in making it.

Start your search by obtaining a list of nursing homes from your local or state ombudsman program. You can locate them by calling the Eldercare Locator. The ombudsman program is a free federal program that investigates problems related to nursing home patient care and protects the rights of nursing home patients.

Since you will probably want to visit at the nursing home often, you should first investigate nursing homes within a short distance of where you live. Then you can compare them to others and see if being close by is more important than other criteria. Some other considerations might be the amount of privacy they allow, how much they regiment the lives of those in their care, and the activities they provide.

The checklist at the end of this chapter will aid you in comparing nursing homes. There are a few things you should know in order to better use this comparison.

Ideally, you should visit a nursing home more than once and during different times of the day. One visit should be during late morning or midday so you can observe whether people are out of bed. During the afternoon or evening visit you can observe what activities are provided for the residents.

Be sure to make an appointment to speak with the admissions director or administrator. Mention why you are visiting and ask to observe the nursing home's daily routine. The administrator can arrange for you to speak with the staff, including the nursing home social worker. You should request a residents' bill of rights (by law, this should be posted). You can ask for a copy to take home.

Also ask to see the nursing home's most recent Medicare or Medicaid survey of the facility and the resulting plan of correction if problems were reported. This list is produced yearly by your state health departments.

As you tour the facility, talk with residents to ascertain their opinion of the nursing home. Be observant and trust your feelings. Make notes of your observations and impressions soon after you leave the facility. Important questions to ask:

• *Does the facility have vacancies, or is there a waiting list?* If there is a waiting list, what is the anticipated time span before accepting new residents?

• *Is the nursing home certified for participation in Medicare or Medicaid programs?* Not all nursing homes accept Medicare or Medicaid patients. If your care recipient needs custodial care, Medicare will not pay for it. In order to receive help from the Medicaid program, your care recipient will have to spend his or her assets. The rules differ from state to state, so you should contact your local state Medicaid agency for more information.

• *What are the facility's admission requirements for residents?*

• *What is the profile of the residents the facility serves?* If your care recipient has specific needs, for example, he or she has Alzheimer's disease, you would want to find a nursing home that is equipped to handle such patients, and vice versa; if this is the home's specialty, it may not be appropriate for a person who is not so afflicted.

• *Does the nursing home require that a resident sign over personal property or real estate in exchange for care?*

Once you have visited several homes you will need to make your decision. Remember, however, that your choice of nursing homes may be somewhat limited by your resources. Financing nursing home care is a major concern to many people—it can cost from $30,000 to $80,000 per year. There are several ways these costs may be financed:

Personal resources. About half of all nursing facility residents initially pay for costs out of personal resources. Because of the high cost of such care, however, many people quickly deplete their resources and apply for Medicaid. See chapter seven for a full discussion of long-term care insurance.

Medicaid. State and federal coverage is available to eligible low-income individuals who need nursing home care at least above the level of room and board. *The nursing home must be Medicaid-certified.*

Medicare. Under some limited circumstances, Medicare (Part A) will pay for a fixed period of skilled nursing home care. The nursing home must be Medicare-certified. Medicare pays only about 2 percent of all nursing home costs. In fact, the most Medicare will cover fully is twenty days, and this is only for skilled nursing care. Many nursing homes have both Medicare and non-Medicare sections. Medicare law does not permit payment for residents in a non-Medicare section of the facility, even if the care needed meets the medical standards for coverage. Therefore, in order for Medicare to pay, the resident must be placed in the section of the nursing home that is certified under Medicare. If Medicare is paying for skilled care for the recipient, then Medicare supplement insurance will also pay. *Reminder: Medicare does not pay for custodial (long-term) care.* Be sure to check with the nursing home as to where your care recipient is being placed.

Veterans' benefits. The Veterans' Administration provides some long-term care for the elderly, but it is extremely limited. When space is available, any veteran or spouse may be eligible for care, even if the need for long-term care has nothing to do with any service-related activity.

When you have completed your nursing home checklist comparison, you should review the contract from your chosen nursing home. Because the admissions contract is a legally binding document, you should talk to a lawyer, if possible, about contract terms. If you have questions, call your Legal Assistance for Seniors. A nursing home contract should include the following:

* the rights and obligations of the resident and grievance procedures

* the rate per day (or month)

* a list of prices for items not included in the basic monthly or daily charges

* the facility's policy on holding a bed if the resident temporarily leaves the home for reasons such as hospitalization

* confirmation as to whether the facility is Medicaid and Medicare certified. If so, the nursing home must accept Medicaid payments when your funds run out, or accept Medicare payments if the care recipient qualifies for that coverage

Before moving your care recipient to a nursing home, it is a good idea to prepare him or her for the moving-in process. Find out if the home has orientation hours when you can bring the prospective resident for a visit. Then the two of you can visit together, which will relieve some of the anxiety you both may have.

Regardless of how well the facility has been selected and no matter how carefully you have discussed the decision with your care recipient, the first day can be traumatic for you both. The moving process and the stay in the nursing home will be easier if you plan ahead.

Some hints that will lessen the trauma:

- Take along some personal items for your care recipient. These may help lessen his or her feeling of loneliness.

- During the move-in, discuss what is happening openly and honestly. Use tact and understanding to reassure him or her, and yourself.

- Be prepared for a lengthy admission process. Most facilities recommend that you plan to arrive around midmorning and expect to spend the day for a smooth transition.

- Eat a meal with the resident, meet the roommate(s), and just be there as your care recipient becomes familiar with the surroundings.

- Before leaving, plan your next visit with the resident. Arrange for phone contact between you in the meantime.

Having done the above, you will have increased the likelihood of social adjustment for the person entering the home. You will also have eased the way for your own adjustment to the change.

TAKING CARE OF YOURSELF

Being a caregiver can take its toll on you. You can not control your loved one's fate by sacrificing yourself. You must nurture and take care of yourself in order to take care of someone else.

Caregivers have numerous misconceptions about their role. One of these is that we can do anything if we try hard enough. However, no matter how much we would like to make things better for someone else, it is not always a realistic goal. Other misconceptions are:

- *We are totally responsible for our care recipient's health and happiness.* This is a natural feeling, but unrealistic. We are only responsible for our own happiness and our own health.

- *If we don't do it no one else will.* It is more probable that if we do it no one else will. We must learn to call on others for help.

- *We can expect love and respect in return for caring.* The care recipient will not love you just because you are giving care.

Caring for someone with a chronic long-term illness puts the primary caregiver at risk for both physical and emotional problems. Physical and mental exhaustion, lack of exercise, poor nutrition, and loss of sleep are common. Nurturing yourself is essential. The following are ways to help you take care of yourself and deal with your stress.

- Encourage and accept help from others.

- Invite family and friends to visit.

- Stay in touch with others through telephone calls and letters.

- Accept that there are times when you may feel angry, hurt, or sad.

- Don't expect perfection from yourself.

- Give yourself credit for what you accomplish.

- Make time to exercise, meditate, read, take a walk, or participate in an activity that gives you pleasure.

- Seek help if you cannot deal with your personal problems.

After you decide which of the above suggestions will work for you, begin to act on them. You will then be on the way to taking care of yourself. If your first choices don't work, try others that might.

Another way to take care of yourself is to join or form a support group. A support group can be a source of comfort as well as a place to share information, caregiving hints, and relief from the social isolation and frustration of in-home caregiving. Some support groups are run by caregivers themselves. The group decides on the format of the meetings and makes its own arrangements for outside speakers or activities.

Other groups are led by professionals, such as social workers or mental health personnel. Some groups meet for a designated period of time, while others are ongoing with people joining and leaving according to their needs. Those led by professionals are more likely to be time-limited. Each caregiver should choose the kind of group that fits his or her needs. The respite from caregiving that the support group provides can be as important as the information and skills that are shared. It is a time to relax, realize you are not alone, and share feelings and solutions with others. If you cannot find a support group in your area and want to start a self-help group, see the resources section at the end of this book.

WHEN YOUR CARE RECEIVER'S LIFE IS TERMINAL

When the person you care for is terminally ill, a range of emotions from depression and fear to anger are predictable and natural. It is possible to have feelings of guilt for wishing to be relieved of the burden of care or to blame yourself for not being able to prolong the life of the person who is dying. A spouse may feel sad about a future filled with loneliness.

Though modern methods often alleviate the suffering of a terminal illness, you may be concerned that the person you are caring for will die in pain. You may worry about your ability to handle the situation as the end approaches or dread being alone at home with your care recipient when he or she dies. You may also fear not recognizing that your patient has died, or you may be worried about what to do when death occurs.

Simply recognizing the presence of these emotions is useful.

Discussing these concerns with a trusted friend, family member, religious advisor, or a social worker or other professional may help.

If a hospice is involved in the dying process, you should discuss your fears with the hospice social worker who will visit with you and the care recipient. (Remember, anyone who is covered by Medicare can receive hospice services with little or no cost.)

Another issue is the right of the dying person to say how he or she wants to live out their last days. One way to protect that right is with an advance medical directive, which is sometimes referred to as a living will or a durable power of attorney for health care. A *durable power of attorney* for health care allows one person to appoint another person, such as a family member or friend, as their agent to make health care decisions for them if they become unable to make those decisions on their own. The appointee may make all decisions related to their health care, subject only to the limitations specified in the document. This document only becomes effective when the patient cannot speak for himself or herself. A *living will* differs from a power of attorney for health care because the person executing a living will gives directions for their future medical care, while a durable power of attorney appoints an agent to make decisions for them. Not all states honor living wills, but all states authorize some type of health directive.

Some durable power of attorney forms include a living will. If you cannot locate such a dual document, you may want to execute both a durable power of attorney and a living will.

The person executing these documents might want to discuss his or her decisions with the person acting as his or her agent. If the appointee is uncomfortable with the written desires, they may be unable to carry them out. In this case it would be advisable to look for a different agent.

The above documents will protect people who want to refuse certain kinds of or all medical treatment. It will also protect those who want all possible treatments to prolong life. Hospitals, nursing homes, some state medical associations, and stationary stores have copies of these documents. The documents differ by state, so be sure the ones you obtain are for the state in which you live.

If the person you have been caring for has stated in a durable power of attorney that they do not want to be resuscitated, some organizations, such as the AARP, suggest that you not call 911 immediately when he or she dies. This is because most areas require paramedics to attempt resuscitation (although these rules are being changed in many places). To further avoid the possibility of resuscitation, wait awhile before calling the coroner or physician.

When your care recipient dies call a friend or relative, when you're ready, who can then contact the following for you, as appropriate:

- the hospice, if you have been using their service

- the care-recipient's physician

- a mortuary, if you have made plans with one

- the county coroner

- your clergyman

Don't hesitate to ask for support at this time. You may be overwhelmed with all kinds of feelings. The following suggestions might help you deal with your immediate grief:

- Ask someone to spend the night with you.

- Have someone go with you to make the funeral plans if they were not done in advance. (If your care receiver was a U.S. veteran, burial at no charge may be possible in a national veterans' cemetery.)

- Have a friend or relative make the calls to those you want notified of the death.

- Have someone keep records of phone calls, letters, flowers, and so on that will have to be acknowledged when you feel up to it.

- Have someone help you when you are ready to dispose of your care recipient's clothes.

When you are ready, also ask someone to help you with the practical details that will need to be taken care of:

- *Find all important papers,* such as a will, trusts, bankbooks, records of investments, and so on.

- *Contact a lawyer.* If you don't have one, get a referral from a friend or relative. Legal Assistance for Seniors may be able to advise you or at least give you some recommendations. Be sure you discuss fees before hiring any attorney. Take a trusted friend or relative with you to the initial meeting so there will be no misunderstanding as to what the attorney will do for you or what their services will cost. Do not make any decisions until you feel emotionally able.

- *Make a substantial number of certified copies of the death certificate.* These may be needed as you make claims against any joint accounts, life insurance payouts, and so on.

- *Notify Social Security of the death.* Depending on the time of the month your care recipient died, you may have to return his or her last Social Security check. There may be changes in the amount of Social Security you will receive. A small burial benefit should be due.

- *Notify all creditors of the death.* Notify any joint credit card issuer. Request that the cards be reissued in your name.

- *Notify your bank and ask them to transfer joint funds to a new account to handle funds received after the death.*

- *If there is a life insurance policy, notify the insurer of the death.*

If your care recipient was a veteran, notify the VA. Find out if you are entitled to any benefits.

BUILDING A NEW LIFE

When your care recipient dies, you will feel grief, despair, and isolated. If you have been a long-term caregiver, you may also feel relief. For months or even years, your life has centered on a routine that is now over. The energy you used in your job as caregiver must now be rechanneled.

The pain you are feeling is normal. Give yourself time to mourn. Indulge yourself—do what you like on your own schedule. "Most people who work with the bereaved agree it takes at least a year for the major part of grief to resolve, and that complete recovery is likely to take two to three years." (Harriet Cooperman, *Dying at Home,* p.118)

Move on at your own pace. Take time to care for or restore your health. Join a bereavement support group. It helps to talk with others who are undergoing the same kind of experience. Most of all, be patient with yourself. Do the things that make you feel better. If you take care of yourself, grief will lessen and you will find your way.

HOME CARE PLANS

Choose the column that fits your situation.

Low Income (Entitled to public assistance)	Limited Income (Able to purchase some assistance	Sufficient Income
1. Determine your assistance needs.	1. Determine your assistance needs.	1. Hire a care manager.
2. Contact your Area Agency on Aging to learn what free services are available to you. Also contact the Eldercare Network, 1-800-677-1116.	2. Contact your Area Agency on Aging to learn what services are available to you. Also contact the Eldercare Network, 1-800-677-1116.	2. The care manager will work with you to determine your needs and create a plan of services.
3. Contact the suggested free services for assistance.	3. Contact the suggested free services for assistance.	3. The care manager will procure services for you.
4. Get commitments of help from family, friends, and neighbors.	4. Ascertain what other services you can afford to pay for.	4. Get commitments of help from family, friends, and neighbors.
	5. Interview applicants for these services. Hire help and keep payroll records.	
	6. Get commitments of help from family, friends, and neighbors.	
	Or	
	5. Choose an employee from an agency that will screen applicants for you and keep employee payroll records.	
	6. Get commitments of help from family, friends, and neighbors.	

Note: If your care recipient has long-term care insurance that covers in-home services, the insurance company may have the right to choose a care manager. Contact the insurance company before hiring an employee or an agency.

EMPLOYMENT CONTRACT

Employment Contract Between
Employer_____ and Employee_____
Employee's Social Security Number_____
If employee is self-employed, please sign here_____

Schedule
Days of work_____
Hours of work: From_____ To_____
Changes in schedule should be negotiated in advance.

Salary
Salary: $_____ per hour / week/ month (circle one)
Terms of salary payment: weekly / monthly (circle one)
Fringe benefits:_____

Duties
Duties to be performed (list all tasks)_____
_____
_____

Household tasks_____
_____
_____

Personal care tasks for care recipient_____
_____
_____

Medical tasks for care recipient_____
_____
_____

Termination
Behavior that will merit termination of this contract_____
_____

Employer's Signature	*Employee's Signature*
Date_____	Date_____
Address_____	Address_____
Phone_____	Phone_____

Nursing Home Checklist

This checklist is designed to help you evaluate and compare the nursing homes you visit. It would be a good idea to make several copies of this checklist for each home you visit. After you have completed checklists on all the nursing homes you plan on visiting, compare your checklists. Comparisons will be helpful in selecting the nursing homes that might be the best choice for you.

Part I—Basic Information

Name of Nursing Home_____

Phone_____

Cultural/Religious Affiliation (if any)_____

Medicaid certified?   __Yes   __No

Medicare certified?   __Yes   __No

Admitting new residents?   __Yes   __No

Convenient location?   __Yes   __No

Capable of meeting your special care needs? __Yes   __No

For parts two through five, rate the nursing home on a scale of one to ten, with ten being a perfect score.

Part II—Quality of Life

1. Are residents treated respectfully by staff at all times?

       1 2 3 4 5 6 7 8 9 10

2. Are residents dressed appropriately and well-groomed?

       1 2 3 4 5 6 7 8 9 10

3. Does staff make an effort to meet the needs of each resident?

       1 2 3 4 5 6 7 8 9 10

4. Is there a variety of activities to meet the needs of individual residents?

       1 2 3 4 5 6 7 8 9 10

5. Is the food attractive and tasty? (Sample a meal, if possible.)
    1 2 3 4 5 6 7 8 9 10
6. Are residents rooms decorated with personal articles?
    1 2 3 4 5 6 7 8 9 10
7. Is the facility's environment homelike?
    1 2 3 4 5 6 7 8 9 10
8. Do common areas and residents rooms contain comfortable furniture?
    1 2 3 4 5 6 7 8 9 10
9. Does the facility have a family and residents' council?
    1 2 3 4 5 6 7 8 9 10
10. Does the facility have contact with outside groups of volunteers?
    1 2 3 4 5 6 7 8 9 10

Part III—Quality of Care

11. Does staff encourage residents to act independently?
    1 2 3 4 5 6 7 8 9 10
12. Does facility staff respond quickly to calls for assistance?
    1 2 3 4 5 6 7 8 9 10
13. Are residents and family involved in resident care planning?
    1 2 3 4 5 6 7 8 9 10
14. Does the home offer appropriate therapies (physical, speech, etc.)?
    1 2 3 4 5 6 7 8 9 10
15.Does the nursing home have an arrangement with a nearby hospital?
    1 2 3 4 5 6 7 8 9 10

Part IV—Safety

16. Are there enough staff to appropriately provide care to residents?
    1 2 3 4 5 6 7 8 9 10
17. Are there handrails in the hallways and grab bars in bathrooms?
    1 2 3 4 5 6 7 8 9 10
18. Is the inside of the home in good repair and exits clearly marked?
    1 2 3 4 5 6 7 8 9 10

19. Are spills and other accidents cleaned up quickly?

    1 2 3 4 5 6 7 8 9 10

20. Are the hallways free of clutter, and are they well-lighted?

    1 2 3 4 5 6 7 8 9 10

Part V—Other Concerns

21. Does the home have outdoor areas (patios, etc.) for resident use?

    1 2 3 4 5 6 7 8 9 10

22. Does the home provide an updated list of medical references?

    1 2 3 4 5 6 7 8 9 10

23. Are the latest survey reports of residents' rights posted?

    1 2 3 4 5 6 7 8 9 10

24. Other_____

    1 2 3 4 5 6 7 8 9 10

25. Other_____

    1 2 3 4 5 6 7 8 9 10

Comments

_____

_____

_____

Adapted from "Guide to Choosing a Nursing Home," U.S. Dept. of Health and Human Services.

Chapter Seven

WHEN WE NEED CARE:
Expanding Our Options

You must do the thing you think you cannot do.
—Eleanor Roosevelt

NOT TOO LONG AGO, we had much shorter life expectancies than now. Although most of us can now look forward to many "bonus" years to enjoy, longer life has added a period in our lives that leaves us more vulnerable to being alone, frail, and to needing assistance.

Until recently, most women believed there would always be a man in their life to care for them, but women now outlive men by almost seven years, and divorce has increased dramatically in our lifetime. Also, a larger percentage of women never married than in previous generations. Thus, less than 30 percent of older women can count on a spouse to be there when they need care.

Another common assumption is that when we need care we can look to our children for help. Unfortunately, many families have experienced changes that limit the resources for care.

Historically, daughters have been the caretakers of their aging parents, but the majority of our daughters are now in the workforce. Many are divorced and often are single parents; others are having children later in life. These daughters find it difficult enough to juggle the complexities of a career and homemaking without having the extra responsibility of caring for one or both of their aging parents. If we have sons, and they are part of a dual-employed household, they are needed to help raise their children and share household responsibilities. Also, many sons believe caretaking is a woman's job. When a son is involved in caregiving it is usually to assist financially or as a care manager.

In addition, due to a high rate of job mobility, many children and their aging parents live thousands of miles apart. Even if they want to, many of these children cannot accept the responsibility of their parents' care. Those who try usually become burned out by the triple burden of career, child raising, and trying to care for their parents. Also, because we are living much longer, many women have children who are also older and who may have chronic illnesses themselves.

Thus children caring for aging parents is no longer realistic. Also, one in five older women will either be childless or will survive her offspring. Therefore, we will have to find new ways to attain the goal of most older women—to age at home and maintain their independence.

There is no one way to accomplish this goal since no single type of older woman fits us all. There are wide differences between middle- and working-class, rich and poor, white women and women of color, and single and married women. Finding the assistance we need will be a challenge that depends partly on the conditions in our lives, such as income, education, and race, as well as our family situations. Also, each of us has established a personal lifestyle that influences our decisions. No matter who we are, most of us will worry about being or becoming dependent on others.

Our society has changed, thus making it ever harder to care for ourselves and avoid dependency. In the past, doctors came to our homes when we were ill, drugstores delivered our prescriptions, grocery stores delivered our food; milkmen delivered our dairy products, vegetable trucks came with fresh fruit and produce, and the postman stopped to chat with us. All of these provided services that now are difficult, costly, or impossible to obtain, and they provided human contact that prevented our isolation and loneliness.

Another difference in our lives is that we are the first generation of women to age since the women's movement. Some of us have carried a feminist perspective into our later years. We believe in ourselves and in our ability to take care of ourselves and to solve our problems. We see independence as a measure of our self-worth. Contrary to popular belief, more than 50 percent of adults over eighty live independently and care for themselves totally. Others, however, face problems of increasing frailty. Learning how to locate, ask for, and accept assistance, as well as how to pay for such assistance, will be imperative.

If we are willing and able to plan for the future, to accept some changes in our lives, to discover what help is available, and to help one another, our hope of aging "in place," that is, at home, and retaining our autonomy may be possible.

YOUR CARING SUPPORT SYSTEM

Families, when we have them, make up part of our support system. We can probably count on them for aid when we have a short-term crisis. Because our children's lives are already burdened, we should not count on them over a long period or for all of our care. The number of children we have and their availability probably will determine the degree of help we can receive. Our children's family situation and financial status as well as other obligations will affect how much help they can offer. If we require too much of their help it may cause them to become exasperated or even desperate over how to care for us.

Some of the people who could be part of our support system are our brothers and sisters. Siblings can well understand our needs because they have shared our experiences throughout a lifetime. As people age, many times sibling relations grow in importance; brothers and sisters may become each other's main support. It is not unusual for siblings to move in together to share their finances and to help with each other's care. Older women have more siblings available than husbands. According to Elizabeth Huttman in *Social Services for the Elderly*, eight out of ten elders have a living sibling, although less than half of elder women have a husband.

Neighbors can be an important part of your support network. When asked, they may pick up your groceries and mail, check on your safety, or possibly take you to the doctor. In senior housing and apartment buildings it is possible to create a buddy system. In a buddy system, you and your buddy become responsible for a daily check-in with each other, by phone or in person. Even those who do not live nearby can be phone buddies. There is something very comforting in knowing that someone will check each day to make sure you are OK. Some hospitals have volunteers who will provide check-up phone calls each day.

When looking for support, don't forget the network of friends you have built throughout your lifetime. Friends can visit, call on the phone, take you for an outing, and in general just keep you from feeling isolated and lonely.

Be creative when thinking about your support network. Use the help of your grown grandchildren, or even nieces and nephews. Also, don't forget to call on those from your church or temple. Most important, start to build a network of support before you need it. Be a friend in need now, and that person will return the help when you need it.

APPRAISING YOUR NEEDS

Most of us, as we age, will need some assistance, if only for someone to give us a ride to the senior center so we can socialize and have a nutritious lunch. Identify your needs and then survey your resources to determine what your family and friends and others in your informal support system can provide. Do you need financial help, transportation, housekeeping help, nursing help, or just emotional support? Do you need to change your living arrangements? We should assess the amount of assistance we need at a given time and seek only that amount of help. This year it may be a little, next year it may be more.

MATCHING YOUR NEEDS AND YOUR RESOURCES

Since resources are limited we will need to use them wisely. We can avoid overusing our informal support system by matching our needs and the formal support services available to us. (Government and purchased services are usually referred to as formal support systems. Family and friends are referred to as our informal support system.)

If possible, when your informal support system cannot provide for your needs, have an assessment by a professional care manager (also referred to as a care coordinator). If you are entitled to receive help at home under a government program for low-income seniors on Medicaid and SSI (see below for an explanation of these programs), that program will do an assessment for you. If you are not eligible, it is still worth the cost of $50 to $75 per hour to have a needs assessment by a private care manager or care coordinator, if one is available. They will help you determine what help you need and what you can afford. They can also help to locate needed services, which is very useful since the availability of services differs from area to area, and they will know about the services in your locale. Additionally, they can coordinate delivery of services.

Involve your family and friends in this assessment if they are willing and available. It is important not to let your family take on a larger burden than they can handle. They should not be made to feel guilty if they cannot do everything for you. If you can get some formal help, your children will more likely be available to give you some of the emotional support you need or perhaps offer financial help to purchase services.

Your task will not necessarily be easy. Many women say they have found they possess too many financial assets to qualify for free or subsidized services, but too few financial resources to purchase services. Therefore, it will take some creativity to accomplish the goal of remaining independent.

Support Services

Living at home may be possible with the help of minimal formal and informal support services. You may need only one service, such as home-delivered meals, to remain independent. If you are alone or less healthy, you will probably need more services. Whether you qualify for government-funded services or whether you can purchase services will depend on your income.

As you consider these services, you should consider: Is this service available near you? What does each service cost? Can it be paid by Medicare, Medicaid, or your insurance? If not, can you afford it? Do you have a family member or friend who could provide the service for you?

The following are some of the formal support services you might consider.

Adult day care offers services such as: meals, activities, a chance to socialize, and assistance with daily living tasks; some centers offer medical services and the assistance of a social worker. Most offer van service to pick you up at home. If you feel isolated in your home, you may want to consider this service. Adult day-care services are usually covered by long-term care insurance. This service can cost $50 to $100 per day. However, there may be a sliding scale and coverage under Medicaid.

An emergency alert system for your home allows you to summon aid by pushing a button on a device, usually worn around your neck, that alerts a central monitoring station. The station then notifies a designated person or calls 911. This is a wonderful safety system for people who live alone. Some hospitals rent these devices. The rental cost is usually around $35 per month.

Home health aides provide personal care services such as cleaning wounds, changing bandages, giving injections, or inserting catheters. Fees run from $10 to $15 per hour depending on the area you live in. The average cost per visit in 1993 was $46. This may be available free of charge for seniors with limited incomes. Contact the state social services department for information.

Nurses and other health care professionals are available through the Visiting Nurses Association, and the charge for a home visit is from $30 to $70 per hour. The average home care visit in 1993 was $84. This may be covered under your state Medicaid program. If you have a long-term care insurance policy, be sure to check whether you are covered for this service.

Medical equipment can be leased or purchased from a hospital or equipment store. Some area agencies like the Red Cross and the American Cancer Society lend these. Hospice programs for the terminally ill cover the cost of medical equipment.

Transportation services vary. Check with your senior center or Department of Aging for taxi scrip. (These are vouchers to help pay for transportation to such places as physicians' offices.) Some cities sell discount tickets for public transportation. Some medical centers have vans to pick up seniors for medical visits. These services vary widely by community. Ask your doctor's office or medical center whether this service is available to you.

Homemaker services include shopping, cooking, and cleaning. These services are available through home health agencies, which should be listed in the yellow pages. This service is invaluable for those who are physically impaired and unable to cook and clean and wish to remain at home. Costs will vary by community. The average 1993 expense per visit was $44. This service may be available free to seniors with limited incomes. Contact your state social services department.

Churches sometimes have "friendly visitors" or telephone callers who will visit with you in person or by phone. This service will be free.

Live-in students or live-in helpers can assist with chores. In exchange for free rent, this person can do some household chores and provide personal support and companionship. Many seniors have found this to be a workable solution to their need for assistance. Many times, this offered the unexpected result of a newfound friend.

In-home support services are programs to help you remain at home if you have a limited income and receive Medicaid and Supplemental Security Income (SSI). The services offered will depend on your needs. Contact your Medicaid office and request in-home support services. Entitlement to these services will vary from state to state.

Meals on Wheels are inexpensive, nutritious meals that can be delivered to your home. If you have transportation, you may want to consider having lunch at a senior nutrition site, which is usually at your senior center or religious center. This will also allow you to socialize and participate in other activities at the center, such as exercise classes, card playing, or movies. A donation is usually requested for meals.

The Friendly Visitor Program was designed to decrease social isolation of those who are homebound. Check with your local office on aging to locate such a program in your area. If this service is available, it will be free.

Telephone reassurance is offered by volunteers who arrange to talk to you daily to make sure you are safe. When available, this service is free and can be located through your Area Agency on Aging.

Many of the above services entail allowing a stranger to come into your home. Before hiring anyone, be sure to investigate the following:

- Have you checked the references of the agency you are considering hiring?

- Have you checked the references of any individual you are considering hiring?

- Has the person you are thinking of hiring been trained to do the service you need?

- Is the person you are hiring to be paid directly or through the agency who sent him or her?

- Does the agency bond its employees?

Additional questions you should consider and a sample employment contract can be found in chapter six.

Alternative Options

No matter what resources are available, there may come a time when you find you are no longer able to remain in your home. At this time, residential care programs such as assisted living or life-care facilities may provide independence and support.

If none of the above options fill your needs, you may want to consider a nursing home. A nursing home (also referred to as institutional care) is an alternative for those who need extended custodial care but not hospitalization. Although it may not be a choice you wish to make, it may be the only kind of care available to meet your needs. Nursing home residents may receive nursing services, room and board, supervision, therapeutic and rehabilitation services, as well as custodial care. Custodial care is for those who require room and board and assistance with personal care but don't necessarily need health care services. Usually you would have access to social and recreational programs, as well. However, since only 5 percent of the population over sixty-five are in nursing homes, your chances are very good that you too will be able to live your life outside of an institution. Actually, 75 to 80 percent of elders are in relatively good health and able to function independently.

If you need custodial care, usually referred to as long-term care, Medicare will probably not pay any of the costs for your care inside or outside of a nursing home. Today's nursing homes usually cost from $30,000 to as much as $80,000 per year, depending on the area you live in. If your assets are limited and you will need help with nursing home costs, it is important to choose one that is Medicaid-certified. After you have put most of your assets toward your nursing home coverage, Medicaid will pay the difference between your income and the cost of long-term care. More than 60 percent of all nursing home care is paid for by Medicaid. The Medicaid program, funded by state and government monies, is administered on a state level, so different eligibility rules apply in different states. Contact Social Security at 1-800-772-1213 for more information and to learn where and how to apply for Medicaid.

How Will You Pay for Your Care?

If you have gone through life being the person who is always there to help someone when they need help, and you suddenly find yourself in the position of having to accept help—whether from family, friends, professionals, community, or government programs—it can be a shock you are ill prepared for. It can require a major adjustment in your habits, in the way you relate to other people, and in your perception of yourself. The adjustment can be distressing. Discussing your situation with a professional or a friend may help you define your situation so that you can figure out what will work best for you and how to finance your care.

Some of the ways we pay for care when we need it is with savings, investments, Social Security and Supplemental Security Income, Medicaid, life insurance, and financial assistance from family members. If you own your home, another way to pay for care is a home equity loan or a reverse mortgage, which is discussed in chapter four. Another way to provide needed capital is to purchase a long-term care policy (see below).

Life insurance "with living benefits" allows you to draw upon the cash value of your life insurance policy to pay for your long-term care. Since there are various types of these policies, be cautious and consult an attorney or financial planner who is familiar with this type of insurance. Even if you have a different type of life insurance, ask the company to buy your equity out. They may not, but it is worth a try since some insurance companies are doing it.

Medicaid is a public assistance program, based on income eligibility, that pays for long-term care in a nursing home, as well as some in-home care and some community-based programs as well as health care. Eligibility and rules differ from state to state, so contact your local Social Security office.

Long-term care insurance is specifically designed to pay for long-term care. This care is usually referred to as custodial care; that is, when someone needs assistance with activities of daily living such as eating, bathing, walking, and toileting. Long-term care policies cover the need for help with activities of daily living as well as help for dementia and Alzheimer's disease patients. Some policies pay for institutional care, such as nursing homes and board and care homes, as well as in-home care. These are called comprehensive policies. Some policies only cover institutional care (nursing homes), while others only cover in-home care. Most elders will need some type of in-home care; fewer people will need institutional care.

People who live to be very old are more apt to need long-term care services than those who die younger. Women are more likely to need these services because of their longer life expectancy. Also, women have more chronic diseases that impair mobility, such as arthritis and osteoporosis, than men. More women will therefore need assistance with activities of daily living, such as bathing, walking, and dressing.

Those who do not have a family support system may want to consider a long-term care insurance policy that will provide some financial help toward purchasing long-term care services or toward paying for nursing home care. However, if you do not have someone who can oversee those you hire to help with your care, and to augment those services you are able to purchase, staying at home may not be possible. You might want to consider an assisted living facility or other type of alternative housing where you can receive the assistance you need. There may come a time, though, when you will need even more care than an assisted living facility can provide. At this point you would have to consider a nursing home if the facility you are in does not have a nursing home component. You should check how any facility you are considering is licensed before deciding to move in. If you purchase a comprehensive long-term care policy, to be sure that it will pay for an assisted living facility or in-home care as well as care in a nursing home.

Unless you have a lot of assets to protect, it may not be wise to purchase a long-term care policy. Consider whether you will be able to make the payments if the premiums continue to rise. If you have a spouse, consider whether you will have enough income to continue to make the payments if he should die.

If you think a long-term care policy fits your needs, you should know that because premiums are based on age, the older you are the higher your premium will be. Many companies restrict the sale of long-term care policies to one-year coverage for those over eighty. Also, very few companies will sell a policy to anyone over eighty-four. Most companies will not give you coverage if you have had an acute illness. It is, therefore, important to plan ahead and purchase such a policy, if you can afford it, as early as possible.

The following are some suggestions adapted from the Trainer's Manual of the Health Insurance Counseling and Advocacy Program, California Department of Aging, of things you should look for in a long-term care policy:

* pays at least $100 a day in benefits for nursing home care

* guarantees a minimum policy duration of two to three years

* pays a home care benefit of $70 to $100 a day

* provides a home care benefit for a wide range of services, including custodial care provided by home health aides, homemakers, or chore workers, without requiring skilled services to qualify

* requires impairment of no more than two activities of daily living, including mental or cognitive impairment

* checks applicant's medical records and history at the time of application

* waives premiums while benefits are being received

* contains inflation protection compounded for the life of the policy

* includes a nonforfeiture premium value (refunding a portion of the premiums paid if the holder cancels the policy after a number of years). You should weigh the value of this benefit before purchasing, because it is very costly.

If you already have a long-term care policy that is more than five years old, you should review it and probably upgrade it, if you can, to remove gatekeepers (things written into the policy to make it hard for you to ever collect) to receiving benefits. One of the most important gatekeepers to try to remove is the requirement for a three-day hospital stay before entering a nursing home in order to trigger benefits.

Most people who enter a nursing home for long-term care do so because they need help with activities of daily living. Therefore, they are not in a hospital prior to entering a nursing home, and the insurance company will not pay for their care. For help in understanding your long-term care policy or in choosing a policy, contact your state health insurance counseling office. There is no charge for this service. If you have trouble reaching your counseling office, call the Medicare hot line at 1-800-638-6833. The state health counseling office is also listed in the front of the U.S. Department of Health and Human Services booklet, "Your Medicare Handbook."

Supplemental Security Income (SSI) is a program for people sixty-five and over whose income is so low that they remain below the poverty level even with their Social Security payment. The federal government, in conjunction with the states, provides a supplement to their income. The amount of the supplement is calculated in terms of various sources of income, including Social Security. This source of assistance is also available for the small group of elderly not eligible for Social Security. It is a means-tested program; the applicant must provide evidence of assets and income. However, there are certain assets—such as your car, a limited amount of savings, and your house—that are not counted in the asset calculation in order to qualify. SSI also allows you to disregard a small amount of earned income.

This program has been underused due to lack of knowledge about it. Many women who are eligible for this benefit do not know it. In some states, if you are an SSI recipient you may also be automatically eligible for Medicaid benefits. In other states you must apply for and establish your eligibility for Medicaid separately. For more information and to find out if you are eligible, contact your local Social Security office. They will help you apply if you are eligible.

The Qualified Medicare Beneficiary Program (QMB) can help with your medical costs if you have a low income and few resources. You can qualify even if you own a home and a car. If you qualify, your state Medicaid program will pay your Part A and B Medicare premiums, the annual deductibles, and other approved Medicare services. You must be sixty-five or older, and you must have Part A Medicare. If you don't already have Part A, but you meet all of the other requirements, such as being over sixty-five and disabled, your Social Security office will help you enroll in Part A. If you already have Part A, contact your state or local welfare, social service, or public health agency. Explain that you may be eligible for the QMB program. Inquire where and when you can fill out an application. Also ask what documents you should bring to document your eligibility. This program could save you hundreds of dollars.

The Older American Act provides funding for programs available to everyone age sixty and older. Services available may (or may not) include: congregate meals, home-delivered meals, case management and assessment, chore services, adult day care, home health care, homemaker services, senior centers, transportation, friendly visiting, and telephone reassurance. Each state allocates the federal funds it receives under the act for programs differently, and each state designates the Area Agency on Aging to provide services directly or through contract with local agencies. There is no charge for services but donations may be accepted. Resources for this program are limited, therefore availability of service is also limited. Contact your Area Agency on Aging to find out what services are available to you.

Family assistance is another way to finance your care. Although it is harder today for family members to give hands-on assistance, many will offer financial support. They may help you purchase long-term care insurance, or they may help pay for assistance in your home. Allowing family members to assist financially may relieve them of feeling guilty when they cannot offer direct care. It may also relieve them of worrying about how you will manage. Most importantly, it may allow you to maintain your independence.

ACCEPTING SUPPORT AND MAINTAINING CONTROL OF YOUR LIFE

When you reach the time that you need care, your children might think it is their responsibility to manage your life. You need to keep communication open within the family and make your wishes and needs known. They cannot give the right amount or even the correct support if they don't know what you need. You will, however, want to remain involved in all of the decisions about your assistance. The more you plan ahead for your own care, the less your family will feel responsible and try to impose solutions on you. It is possible to stay independent but still accept some help. As you would with any friend, be sure to express appreciation for any help your family offers. Also continue to maintain your network of friends so that you will not become too dependent on your children, and use whatever community services are available to you. And only ask for the amount of help you need at the time.

If planning for your own care seems a daunting task, remember that you have taken care of yourself most of your life. This is just another step. Chances are you are capable of handling this. If you plan ahead, become knowledgeable about resources, and give help to others now so that you will feel comfortable in asking for help when you need it, you will be able to maintain a sense of control over your life as well as your care.

Chapter Eight

Facing the End of Life:
Finishing the Journey

Sometime soon the book will be complete
And songs all sung. The day will come
When wisdom will be known and mountains climbed;
The speeches will be said, the biscuits baked,
The loving letters penned.
—Ernestine Hoff Emrick

AT EVERY STAGE OF life's journey, we have faced choices. As we grow older, there is more to look back on and less ahead. But it is the distance ahead that is important now. Now is the chance to summarize in some wise way, to make sense out of it all—one last chance to make a point.

The last chapter of a book also gives us the chance to reinforce or summarize before the reader turns the last page. Because of this, we want to restate our theme, to say again that our lives as older women need to be understood as if we are "whole," not just parts of the whole. Any question, challenge, choice, or change we face as women is affected by and will affect our sense of self, our health, our finances, what we do with our time, where and how we live, how we care for others, and how we get care for ourselves.

THE CHALLENGES WE FACE

The last challenge we face in preparing for the end of life is no different, except the stakes are higher. Our life and our death is the topic here.

Finishing our life's journey is like no other ending we have experienced. Other endings, like graduation from school, ending a marriage, or saying good-bye to a loved one, have a finality to them, but also the possibility—sometimes hidden—to begin again, to go beyond, to re-create ourselves anew. The end of life is different.

The differences we face in preparing for death are powerful, and they shape our feelings and what we do about them.

+ Death is predictable. No matter how devoutly we wish, we cannot live forever. Our existence is finite and therefore unarguable.

+ Our time left to live is unpredictable. The older we become, the closer we are to death, but whether it comes tomorrow or thirty years ahead is unknown to us. Time becomes more precious.

+ Even though death is certain, dying is not. We may loiter or linger much longer than we would wish, becoming increasingly frail, losing our physical, mental, and our emotional ability to live a life of independence, usefulness, and dignity. Or we may die peacefully in our sleep at the end of a fulfilling and joyful day, with no pain or warning.

Whatever scenario is written for our future, there is no doubt that preparing for the end of life is our last major challenge. In earlier times, death was a natural and expected part of life. People of all ages were cared for and died at home among familiar faces. This is no longer usually the case. Dying is not what it used to be. Most of us now die in hospitals or other institutions where death is often out of sight and out of our hands. There is ample evidence that death has become medicalized and institutionalized.

Because of this, there is a growing national debate over who should control decisions about the timing and method of death. New technology as well as legal and economic policies governing medical procedures force us to confront, or at least consider, the possibilities of choice. Even defining a point for ourselves beyond which we cannot conceive of wanting to live is now a possibility. There is surely no consensus among the disciplines of religion, medicine, philosophy, or law about the practical, economic, and ethical controversies involved in this debate.

One of the results of this public debate is our own uncertainty about how to approach death. How can we decide what constitutes for us a "good" death? The question itself raises difficult questions. We may occasionally envision how we hope to die, but most of us worry about what will actually happen to us in the process of dying. Even though aging brings with it the reality that our time left to live is decreasing, talking openly about planning for the end of life has been a taboo, rather than a sanctioned topic. Too often, death is a subject to be evaded, ignored, even denied. However, as new alternatives such as the hospice movement and living wills have gained acceptance, planning for our own death has become more agreeable and less feared. There is ample evidence in the psychological literature to support the effectiveness of preparing for the worst as a strategy for decreasing anxiety over the unknown. For example, planning ahead for possible calamity can help free us to let go of our fear of the future.

EXPERIENCING THE DEATH OF OTHERS

In many cultures, caring for the sick and preparing for and making sense of death is the work of women, especially of old women. Whether or not it's fair or best, women still act as the nurturers, caregivers, and custodians of those near death. The longer we live, the more likely we are to experience the deaths of relatives and friends, those we have come to look to as the anchors of our life. Each time we cross off a name on our address or phone list, we are reminded of our own mortality.

Grieving

Whether a death is anticipated, or comes unexpectedly, coming to terms with the reality of loss is a very real, painful, and personal experience. The process of grieving and answering the question, Why? may become overwhelming. But beyond the initial six-month period of numbness and shock, healing is possible. The trauma of trying to let go of a previous role and adjust to a new one is both a challenge and an opportunity. The challenge, of course, is to grieve as well as to release the guilt, self-blame, anger, anxiety, or overwhelming sadness that can lead to extended depression. Paying attention to our feelings and talking about them with others can be extremely helpful. It may also be useful to get professional help—from a clergyman or counselor—to deal with the process of mourning.

Here are some practical suggestions on how to help a dying or recently bereaved person:

- Listen respectfully to their feelings. Express your own sadness and regret, but do not try to be unnaturally cheerful. Sincere feelings are more appropriate than false ones.

- Extend your support and assistance, but also respect another's need for privacy.

- Send cards or notes or make phone calls if you can't visit.

- Offer specific kinds of help. "Could I get you something from the drugstore?" is easier to accept than a vague offer of help.

Theories such as Elizabeth Kubler Ross's well-known five-stage model may be helpful in dealing with death. She suggests that grieving follows a pattern of successive stages of denial and isolation, anger, bargaining, depression, and acceptance. Though models like this can be helpful and reassuring guides, people do not always pass through these stages in an orderly or predictable fashion. Worrying about not doing it right is an unnecessary added reason for guilt and anxiety. Stages such as this may also be less important to very old people who may believe it is time, or even past time, to die.

Widowhood

Outliving one's spouse is a fact of life for many older women. More than half of all women live alone by age sixty-five, and the number of widows increases dramatically as women grow older and outlive their husbands. This has implications for older women far beyond the obvious fact of living alone. Despite a popular assumption that widows live well from legacies of insurance policies and inheritances, the stereotype of the "merry widow" just isn't the case for the majority of America's millions of widows.

Regardless of age, race, or financial situation, the death of a spouse results in an inescapable return to the old role of single adult and the assumption of a new role, that of a widow. More than any other life event, this transition requires the greatest life readjustment. Widowhood is especially traumatic for a woman who has lived most of her adult life in a secure marriage and has built, over many years, her identity as a wife. The necessity of creating even small, new everyday habits, like what to buy at the grocery store or who will take out the garbage, put gas in the car, or water the garden, can be a traumatic and painful experience.

How women deal with or react to the death of a spouse varies. A marriage may have been difficult, marked by disagreements, conflict, or prolonged illness. Death, when it comes to the very old and frail, may come as a relief to suffering as well as ending prolonged financial and caregiving responsibilities for the survivors. Whatever the circumstances, the ability to move beyond grief and mourning requires time.

Robert C. DiGuilio, in his book *Beyond Widowhood,* suggests that there are many truths about widowhood, but the one essential characteristic of successfully moving beyond that deep, nameless hurting that affects the widowed is the realization that to resume living fully depends solely on the decision of the widowed to do so. Whether the decision is to live a full life—no matter how difficult life has been in the past—perhaps for the very first time, what is involved is *permission* to be happy again.

Joining a self-help or support group for widows can be a great comfort. Such groups help us realize that our feelings are shared by others. Family service agencies, senior centers, and religious organizations commonly offer such services. The AARP Widowed Persons Service is a program in which trained widowed volunteers reach out to the newly widowed. The program includes one-on-one outreach, support groups, and a variety of community education programs. Many have found that this program brings new perspectives, new hope, and perhaps most important, understanding. *On Being Alone,* a guide for widowed persons published by the AARP, advises new widows to be cautious about making irreversible decisions quickly during the initial period of mourning. Decisions such as quitting a job, selling a home, moving in with family members, or moving to a new location are probably best postponed until the consequences of such major choices can be carefully considered.

FACING OUR OWN DYING AND DEATH

Probably no one can ever be fully ready for death, in the sense of knowing about and accepting the experience in advance, but we can prepare ourselves for the emotional and practical challenges involved. Although every practical issue connected to the end of life is complicated by its emotional component, there are some things over which we do have a measure of control. We can learn about options, plan ahead, and take practical steps to assure that our choices will be carried out. Once we have thoughtfully and sensitively done this, our resistance and apprehension about the end of life may be reduced. It has been said that fully facing the worst scenario we can imagine in our future can shift our hidden fears, from anxiety to peace and energy for living.

We have the right to make decisions about our death. Thinking carefully about options for our care, such as the use of medical technology to prolong life or the amount of pain control we want, can reduce some of the powerlessness we often feel about the end of life. We may prefer not to be subjected to complex technological procedures that may extend life a few extra days, weeks, or months at the expense of a quality of life of our choosing. Each of us has a right to accept or refuse medical care and to say whether we wish to die in or outside a hospital.

Advance Medical Directives

Advance medical directives can be stated in a living will or in a durable power of attorney for health care. A living will gives written instructions for your future medical care, stating what you want and don't want. A durable power of attorney for health care is a document in which you appoint a health-care agent or proxy to represent you in the event you become unable to communicate your wishes. The durable power of attorney offers a greater amount of predictable control over decisions about medical treatment options. Either document should be carefully completed, and copies should be accessible to family members and your physician.

An advance medical directive can express your wishes regarding medical care, such as whether you wish to die at home or in a hospital. You can also make arrangements to donate organs, such as kidneys and corneas for transplant purposes, or your entire body for medical research. No matter what your choices are, they must be in writing, in acceptable legal form, and be understood and accessible to all those who may be involved with your care. It is wise to keep a card in your wallet stating that you have advance directives and where they can be found.

For elders who want an alternative to the accepted model of hospitalization until death, hospice programs are now available in many communities. These programs may be located by calling local visiting nurse agencies or hospitals. One of the major goals of a hospice program is to maintain the quality of life outside a traditional hospital for individuals whose life expectancy is six months or less. Trained hospice workers provide spiritual and emotional support, medication, pain management, and temporary relief for caregivers. They also provide trained volunteer visitors, visiting nurses, nurse's aides, homemakers, and bereavement counseling for family and friends. Medicare, Medicaid, and some other insurance plans may pay part of the cost. For a patient to qualify for Medicare hospice benefits, the patient's physician must certify that life expectancy is at a terminal stage.

Planning for Our Survivors

Claiming the right to control the end of our life in no way minimizes the seriousness or the finality of the decisions we make affecting those we leave behind. While it may be difficult to discuss or even to think about, we have the responsibility to complete a will or a trust to clarify and determine what happens to our assets after our death. Without a will or a trust, an entire estate, no matter how big or small, might end up in the hands of the state rather than our family.

Different types of wills, such as handwritten or fill-in-the-blank wills, are legal in some states. However, lawyers are up-to-date on state laws and can help put together a more personalized estate plan.

If a lawyer is unaffordable, you might consider legal service offices and reduced-fee lawyer referral services, which are often accessible through local senior centers.

The process of completing a will or a trust involves more, of course, than just deciding logically and unemotionally how we want our property and possessions distributed. Complex feelings about our family, our friends, and what we really value often cause us to delay the process, thinking that we have time to accomplish the task. We may also worry endlessly about getting every detail right in an effort to please everyone named in the document. Since this objective is unrealistic, a reasonable approach is to view a will or trust as an ongoing document, and not a once-in-a-lifetime creation forever sealed and stored in a secret place. Plans and documents such as this need to be updated when you change your mind about major provisions; when there are important changes in your assets; when there are changes in your family such as a marriage, birth, adoption, divorce, or death; or when new laws require revisions to your plan.

Letters of Instruction

Once you have completed a will or trust, a letter of instruction provides another kind of answer to the question, How can I prepare for the end of my life? Although not a legal document, a letter of instruction is a guide to make it easier for your family, friends, or those you leave behind to know what to do when you die.

A letter of instruction may be written or placed on audiotape or video. It can be lengthy and detailed, or a simple statement expressing your wishes about cremation or burial, or a funeral or memorial service. A thoughtfully prepared statement can be extremely helpful to those who are faced with making the many decisions necessary after your death. Preparing a statement like this can also enable you to get your affairs and thoughts together. When we write something down, we sometimes discover what we really think.

Here is a list of possible information to include in a letter of instruction:

- *A document locator* describing where to find your financial and legal records and documents.

- *A list of names and addresses* of professional advisors such as your attorney, insurance agent, accountant, and so on, and a list of family members and close friends and where they can be found.

- *Funeral or memorial information* listing details of your wishes for burial or cremation and arrangements you have already made, as well as instructions for the type of service you would like. These suggestions are especially helpful for those who have the responsibility of deciding "what Mother would have wanted."

- *Personal property distribution* not covered by a will or trust. Your wishes, including any prior arrangements or promises you have made to family, friends, or organizations for the distribution of personal property.

- *A guide for survivors* describing the details that must be attended to, whether or not any prior arrangements have been made. A publication such as *Final Details: A Guide for Survivors When Death Occurs*, available from the AARP, includes a practical guide.

FINISHING THE JOURNEY

An increasing awareness of our own mortality often pressures us to come to a better understanding of the great, universal transition at the end of life. For some, this stage of life can offer us the opportunity to complete the unfinished business of our life: the chance to reflect on who we were, who we are, and how we want to be remembered. From this perspective, aging does not mark an end, but rather the beginning of making sense of such questions so that our life can have an end.

Reflecting on the past is a natural part of this process, helping us accept our lives: our joys and accomplishments, our mistakes and disappointments. There are numerous ways to reflect, remember, and record life's experiences. Writing or taping memories, or putting together a family album can all be gifts to ourselves and to those we care about—a legacy to the next generation. Creating a scrapbook, even a cookbook of favorite recipes, can be a gift that tells a story. Sharing what we mean to one another, telling each other what the really important things in life are—what we have learned from life and what we would like to be remembered for—gives us and our families a sense of the value of life. There are a variety of publications to guide us through this process. Courses and workshops are often available through senior centers or adult education programs. It is also possible to get together with friends and share ideas for life review projects that "tell our stories."

According to an old saying, as we age, we become more of who we already are. Contemplating who we have been and who we are frees us to live and appreciate the wonder of life. Another wise saying tells us to live our lives forward, since going backward to an earlier time is not possible. Too often we feel that it is too late to plan for the future, to make important changes in ourselves, or to have significant impact on the world around us. Not so. Of course, we can do little about certain events, such as the deaths of those we love, serious accidents or illnesses, financial disasters, earthquakes, and fires. But we can still reorient what is important to us, put our lives in order, and take action to become the kind of elder woman we want to be.

We will, sooner or later, die. The question is, how are we going to live the time we have left? As the days dwindle to a precious few, our dreams for the future are as important as our memories.

We hope this book will help make it possible to live out your life with grace, dignity, peace, and a sense of empowerment over the choices ahead. The travel is both an outer and an inner journey, for the place we enter now is unknown. It may require new values and new directions as yet undiscovered. The "different voice" of women, only now beginning to be heard, may light our way.

I shall be telling this with a sigh
Somewhere ages and ages hence:
Two roads diverged in a wood, and I—
I took the one less traveled by,
And that has made all the difference.
                    —Robert Frost

RESOURCES:
Finding the Help You Need

THROUGHOUT THIS BOOK WE have encouraged readers to stay in control of their lives by planning ahead and being knowledgeable about available assistance. The following list contains names, addresses, and phone numbers of sources to contact for information to supplement that supplied in the rest of this book. Call or write these resources even if you are not sure they can assist you. They may be able to refer you to another person or agency if they cannot assist you directly. Although we have listed national locations, many agencies also have local chapters.

Other resources can be located in your local phone book under government listings. These pages usually list General Information and Referral, Counseling, Death and Dying, Disability Services, Financial Assistance, Medical and Healthcare Assistance, Legal Services, and Social Services. Also check your phone book's yellow pages for a heading such as Senior Services and Organizations. Libraries and religious organizations can also help locate information.

GENERAL INFORMATION AND ASSISTANCE

Administration on Aging
Department of Health and Human Services
330 Independence Avenue SW
Washington, DC 20201
202-401-4541
The central federal agency for aging advocacy and services.

American Association of Retired Persons (AARP)
601 E Street NW
Washington, DC 20049
202-434-2277
Annual membership fee. Free low-cost publications for members on home care, elder abuse, home modification, caregiving, retirement housing, insurance, nutrition, legal and financial issues, Medicare, vision and hearing, Alzheimer's disease, nursing homes, and so on. For catalog of publications, write to 1909 K Street NW, Washington DC 20049.

American Self-Help Clearinghouse
St. Clair's Riverside Medical Center
Denville, NJ 07834
201-625-7101
Book on forming self-help groups.

American Society on Aging
833 Market Street, Suite 511
San Francisco, CA 94103
800-537-9728
Education and training events for professionals in aging. Publications for members.

Catholic Charities, U.S.A.
1731 King Street, Suite 200
Alexandria, VA 22314
703-549-1390
Extensive services for older people include counseling, homemaker services, home health care, and so on.

Children of Aging Parents
1609 Woodbourne Road, Suite 302A
Levittown, PA 29057
800-227-7294
Membership fee. Publications on caregiving, newsletter, and phone counseling.

Department of Veteran's Affairs
800-827-1000
Check local phone listings
Must be eligible. Nursing home care, medical services, burial and death benefits, and eyeglasses. VA hospitals offer medical care, pharmacies, and social services.

Eldercare Locator Service
1112 16th Street NW, Suite 100
Washington, DC 20036
800-677-1116
National guide to finding community support services. Referrals made to local organizations offering services to seniors. Sponsored by Area Agency on Aging.

Episcopal Society for Ministry on Aging
317 Wyandotte Street
Bethlehem, PA 18015
610-868-5400
Programs to meet the spiritual, physical, and mental needs of the elderly. Also, programs to involve homebound persons in community activities.

Medicare
Address varies by zip code
800-638-6833
Counselors available to answer questions on eligibility and enrollment. Referrals to local offices.

National Association of Area Agencies on Aging
1112 16th Street NW, Suite 100
Washington, DC 20036
202-296-8130
List of aging resources in local areas. Location and phone numbers of local offices can be found in the Government listings of local phone books.

National Association of State Units on Aging
1225 I Street NW, Suite 725
Washington, DC 20005
202-785-0707
Organization of all state offices or departments on aging. Information about ombudsman programs, activities, and long-term care. Location and phone numbers of local offices can be found in the Government listings of local phone books.

The National Council on the Aging, Inc.
409 3rd Street SW, Suite 200
Washington, DC 20024
202-479-1200
Information on services and programs in the field of aging.

National Institute on Aging
Public Information Office
Building 31, Room 5C27
31 Center Drive, MSC 2292
Bethesda, MD 20892
301-496-1752
Free publication, "Resource Directory for Older People."

Older Women's League
666 Eleventh Street NW, Suite 700
Washington, DC 20001
800-825-3695
Membership required. Support for midlife and older women in achieving economic and social equity. Seeks to improve the image and status of older women. Referrals to local chapters.

Social Security Administration
Office of Public Inquiries
6401 Security Blvd.
Baltimore, MD 21235
800-772-1213
Information about Social Security, Medicare, and Medicaid. Local offices.

Volunteers of America (VOA)
3939 North Causeway Boulevard
Metairie, LA 70002
504-837-2652
Senior centers and apartments for older people. Referrals for home repair services, homemaker assistance, Meals on Wheels, and transportation. Check phone book for local listing.

BEREAVEMENT, DEATH, AND DYING

Choice in Dying
200 Varick Street
New York, NY 10014
800-989-9455
Publications on pain management, medical treatments, and your living will. Living-will forms for each state by written request.

Concern for Dying
212-528-2971
Information on living wills.
Continental Association of Funeral and Memorial Societies
200 I Street NW, Suite 530
Washington, DC 20009
202-745-0634
Information about alternatives for funeral planning. Information and referral to "memorial societies," nonprofit groups that arrange low-cost funeral services for members.

The Compassionate Friends
P.O. Box 3696
Oakbrook, IL 60522
708-990-0010
Support groups and information for bereaved family members.

Cremation Association of North America
111 East Wacker Drive
Chicago, IL 60601
312-644-6610
Publication on cremation.

Federal Trade Commission
Office of Public Affairs
6th Street and Pennsylvania Avenue NW, Room 421
Washington, DC 20580
202-326-2180
Free publication on FTC funeral rules. Also investigates consumer
complaints. Referral to local offices.

Funeral Service Consumer Arbitration Program
P.O. Box 27641
Milwaukee, WI 53227
800-662-7666
Mediation of disputes between consumers and funeral providers.

The Living Bank
800-528-2971
Information on organ donations.

National Hemlock Association
P.O. Box 11830
Eugene, Oregon 97440
503-342-5748
Information and publications on assisted suicide.

National Funeral Directors Association Learning Resource Center
1121 W. Oklahoma Avenue
Milwaukee, WI 53227
414-541-2500
Free publications on death and dying, embalming, suicide, and so on.

Caregiving and Care Receiving

Aging Network Services
4400 East-West Highway, Suite 907
Bethesda, MD 20814
301-657-4329
National referral service for geriatric care managers.

American Association of Homes and Services for the Aging
901 E Street NW, Suite 500
Washington, DC 20004
202-783-2242
Free caregiving brochure.

American Health Care Association
1200 15th Street NW
Washington, DC 20005
202-833-2050
Publications on nursing homes.

Andrus Gerontology Center
University of Southern California
University Park, MC 0191
Los Angeles, CA 90089
Low-cost brochure on caregiving and elder-care counseling.

Family Service America
11700 West Lake Park Drive
Milwaukee, WI 53224
800-221-2681
Referrals to local Family Service Associations offering counseling, support groups, and assessment to individuals and families.

Foundation for Hospice and Home Care
513 C Street NE
Washington, DC 20002
202-547-6586
Free consumer guides.

Jewish Family Services
No national office; check local phone book
Affordable services such as family counseling, visitors, and care
managers.

Kelly Assisted Living
P.O. Box 332280
Detroit, MI 48232
800-541-9818
Free brochures on home care, Alzheimer's disease, home modifica-
tion, and legal issues.

Long-Term Care Ombudsman
Check with your Area Agency on Aging for local listings.
Investigation of nursing home complaints and advocacy for nursing
home residents or their families.

National Alliance for Caregiving
7201 Wisconsin Avenue, Suite 620
Bethesda, MD 20814
301-718-8444
Information on elder-care conferences, publications, and training for
family and professional caregivers.

National Association for Home Care
228 7th Street SE
Washington, DC 20003
202-547-7424
Guide to choosing home care.

National Association of Professional Geriatric Care Managers
1604 N. Country Club Road
Tucson, AZ 85716
520-881-8008
Referral to care managers in local areas who assess the needs of the
elderly and who arrange and supervise in-home help and services.

National Association of Social Workers
750 1st Street NE, Suite 700
Washington DC 30003
202-408-8600
Counseling and case management.

National Consumers League
1701 K Street, NW, Suite 1200
Washington, DC 30006
202-835-3323
Publications such as *All About Home Care: A Consumers Guide.*

National Family Caregivers Association
9621 East Bexhill Drive
Kensington, MD 30895
301-942-6430
Newsletter, person-to-person network, and educational materials to
support caregivers' quality of life.

National Home Care
519 C Street NE
Washington, DC 20002
202-547-6586
A division of Foundation for Hospice and Home Care, Inc.
Information on hospices and home care.

Nursing Home Information Center
1331 F Street NW
Washington, DC 20004
202-347-8800
Information and referral center for long-term-care consumer services.
Information on nursing homes, alternative community services, and
how to select a nursing home.

National Hospice Organization
1901 N. Moore Street, Suite 901
Arlington, VA 22209
800-658-8898
Information on locating local hospice organizations.

U.S. Department of Health and Human Services
Health Care Financing Administration
7500 Security Boulevard
Baltimore, Maryland 21244
800-638-6933
Booklet and audiocassette, *The Guide to Choosing a Nursing Home*

Visiting Nurse Association of America
3801 East Florida Avenue, Suite 900
Denver, CO 80320
800-426-2547
Free referrals to home health-care providers.

Well Spouse Foundation
610 Lexington Avenue, Suite 814
New York, NY 10022
800-838-0879
Membership open to partners of chronically ill people. Newsletter and local support groups.

FINANCES

American Council of Life Insurance
1001 Pennsylvania Avenue NW
Washington, DC 20004
202-624-2414
or
National Insurance Consumers Helpline
800-942-4242
Information about insurance-related matters. Brochures and fact sheets on insurance, health care, Medicare, long-term care, and support groups.

Consumer Information Center
P.O. Box 100
Pueblo, CO 82002
or
General Services Administration
18th and F Streets NW, Room G142
Washington, DC 20405
202-501-1794
CIC is a department of GSA, which helps government agencies provide the public with information.
Publication, *Consumer Information Catalog,* listing government publications on housing, retirement, benefits, insurance, nutrition, recreation, hobbies, and financial matters.

Council of Better Business Bureaus
Consumer Information
4200 Wilson Boulevard, Suite 800
Arlington, VA 22203
703-276-0100
Investigation of fraudulent and questionable practices that concern older people. Publishes reports and newsletters, pamphlets, and guidebooks.

Institute of Certified Financial Planners
7600 East Eastman Avenue, Suite 301
Denver, CO 80231
800-282-7526
Names and qualifications of three certified financial planners in local areas and copy of brochure, *Selecting a Qualified Financial Planning Professional: Twelve Questions to Consider.*

Insurance Information Institute
110 William Street
New York, NY 10038
800-331-9146
Information about insurance. Recommends sources of information and assists people who have complaints or claims.

National Association of Personal Financial Advisors
1130 West Lake Cook Road, Suite 150
Buffalo Grove, IL 60089
708-537-7722
List of "fee-only" planners in local areas and an interview form to assist in choosing a financial planner, "Questions that could change your financial future."

National Consumers League
1701 K Street NW, Suite 1200
Washington, DC 20006
202-824-3323
Consumer education and distribution of materials on subjects relevant to the elderly. Catalog of publications available.

Pension Rights Center
918 16th Street NW, Suite 704
Washington, DC 20006
202-296-3776
Advocacy for retirees and workers before government agencies. Newsletter and fact sheets on pension issues.

Service Corps of Retired Executives
409 3rd Street SW, 4th floor
Washington, DC 20024
800-634-0245
Information to retirees starting their own businesses. Sets up counseling sessions with retired executives. Recruits qualified retirees as volunteers.

Social Security Administration
Office of Public Inquiries
6401 Security Boulevard
Baltimore, MD 21235
800-772-1213
Estimate of benefits upon request. The SSI provides additional payments to older people already receiving public assistance. Free brochure, *Your Medicare Handbook.*

U.S. Internal Revenue Service
800-829-3676
Free copy of *Tax Information for Older Americans* (Pub. 554).

HEALTH

Alzheimer's Association
919 North Michigan Avenue, Suite 1000
Chicago, IL 60611
800-272-3900
24-hour hot line for information on local support groups and community resources.

American Academy of Ophthalmology
National Eyecare Project.
P.O. Box 7424
San Francisco, CA 94230
800-222-3937
Referrals for medical eye care from practicing ophthalmologists for legal residents and citizens over age sixty-five who have difficulty paying for eye care.

American Association for Geriatric Psychiatry
230 North Michigan Avenue
Chicago, IL 60601
Referrals to geriatric psychiatrists in local areas.

American Cancer Society
1599 Clifton Road NE
Atlanta, Georgia 30329
800-227-2345
Check telephone listings for local chapter. Some have medical equipment for loan, lists of community resources, transportation services, and support groups.

American Council of the Blind
1155 15th Street, NW, Suite 720
Washington, DC 20005
800-424-8666
Information and referrals to local support groups, consumer product guidance, and funding sources.

American Dental Association
Division of Communications
211 East Chicago Avenue
Chicago, IL 60611
312-440-2500
Referrals to state dental associations offering free or low-cost services for elders.

American Diabetes Association
1660 Duke Street
Alexandria, VA 22314
800-232-3472
Information on diagnosis and treatment of diabetes. Local chapters sponsor screening programs, information, support, and referral to community agencies and services.

American Geriatrics Society
770 Lexington Avenue, Suite 300
New York, NY 10021
212-308-1414
List of physicians specializing in the aged.

American Heart Association
7272 Greenville Avenue
Dallas, TX 75231
800-242-8721
Public education programs about heart disease and stroke. Referrals to local affiliates.

American Nurses Association
600 Maryland Avenue SW, Suite 100W
Washington, DC 20024
800-274-4262
List of state nurse associations.

American Occupational Therapy Association
4720 Montgomery Lane
Bethesda, MD 20824
301-652-2682
Computerized database listing adaptive items.

American Parkinson's Disease Association
1250 Hylan Boulevard, Suite 4B
Staten Island, NY 10305
800-223-2732
Referrals to local chapters providing information on community services, physicians, and treatment. Publications.

American Psychiatric Association
1400 K Street NW
Washington, DC 20005
202-682-6220
Referrals to local psychiatrists.

American Red Cross
430 17th Street NW
Washington, DC 20006
202-737-8300
Medical equipment loans in some areas. Local offices listed in phone
book.

Arthritis Foundation
1314 Spring Street NW
Atlanta, GA 30309
800-283-7800
Information, publications, and referrals to support groups.

Better Hearing Institute
P.O. Box 1840
Washington, DC 20013
800-327-9355
Information on hearing loss and hearing aids.

Hearing Aid Helpline
20361 Middlebelt Road
Livonia, MI 48152
800-521-5247
Referral to local support groups, brochures, product information for
hearing aids, and directory of hearing specialists.

Help for Incontinent People
P.O. Box 8310
Spartanburg, SC 29305
800-252-3337
Information and resources for bladder and bowel control problems.
List of physicians and publications.

Medic Alert Foundation
P.O. Box 381009
Turlock, CA 95381
800-344-3226
Information about emergency medical identification system. Provides
ID bracelet, necklace, or wallet card.

National Association for the Visually Handicapped
22 West 21st Street
New York, NY 10010
212-889-3141
Visual aids catalog. Offers a large print lending library by mail.

National Cancer Institute
Cancer Information Service
9000 Rockville Pike
Building 31, Room 10A-24
Bethesda, MD 20892
800-422-6237
Referrals to local support groups and publications.

National Council on Alcoholism and Drug Dependence
12 West 21st Street, 7th floor
New York, NY 10010
800-622-2255
Information, publications, and referrals to local chapters.

National Institute of Mental Health
5600 Fishers Lane, Room 15C-05
Rockville, MD 20892
301-443-4513
Information and assistance.

National Institute of Neurological Disorders and Stroke
Information Office
31 Center Drive, MSC 2540
Building 31, Room 8A06
Bethesda, MD 20892
800-352-9424
Materials on prevention, detection, and treatment of strokes and information about after-care centers and rehabilitation.

National Multiple Sclerosis Society
733 3rd Avenue, 6th Floor
New York, NY 10017
Information and referral to local support groups.

National Register of Health Care Providers in Psychology
1120 G Street NW, Suite 330
Washington, DC 20005
202-783-7663
Listings of psychologists by geographic area and services offered.

National Self-Help Clearinghouse
25 West 43rd Street, Room 620
New York, NY 10036
212-642-2944
Information on self-care and self-help groups, assistance, and referrals.

Parkinson's Disease Foundation
710 West 168th Street
New York, NY 10032
800-457-6676
Information, publications, counseling advocacy, and referrals to physicians.

Stroke Connection of the American Heart Association
7272 Greenville Avenue
Dallas, TX 75231
800-553-6321
Information and referral service for stroke survivors and families. Lists local groups, publishes newsletter, sells books, videos, and literature.

HEALTH INSURANCE

Health Insurance Association of America
555 13th Street NW, Suite 600E
Washington, DC 20004
800-942-4242
Information on health insurance and publications, including *A Consumer's Guide to Medicare Insurance* and *A Consumer's Guide to Long-Term Care Insurance.*

Insurance Counseling and Assistance Program
Check with your Area Agency on Aging for local listings.
Assistance with questions on long-term care and health insurance costs, eligibility, and coverage.

National Insurance Consumer Help Line
800-942-4242
Answers to questions about insurance. Refers complaints to appropriate sources and provides brochures on how to choose an agent or broker and how to select an insurance company.

United Seniors Health Cooperative
1331 H Street NW, Suite 500
Washington, DC 20005
202-393-6222
Consumer reports, newsletter, and books on home and long-term care, insurance, and financing.

HOUSING

Adaptive Environment Center
374 Congress Street, Suite 301
Boston, MA 02210
617-695-1225
Publications and educational programs such as *Consumer's Guide to Home Modification* and *Achieving Physical and Communications Accessibility.*

Assisted Living Facilities Association of America
10300 Eaton Place, Suite 400
Fairfax, VA 22031
703-691-8106
Membership organization for assisted living facilities industry. Also publishes consumer information; send a SASE for a list of publications and informational brochures.

Center for Accessible Housing
North Carolina State University
P.O. Box 8613
Raleigh, NC 27695
919-515-3082
Phone and technical assistance on a wide range of housing needs. Publications on home modification, housemate agreements, and so on.

Conservation and Renewable Energy Inquiry and Referral Service
P.O. Box 8900
Silver Spring, MD 20907
800-523-2929
Funded by the U.S. Department of Energy. Wide variety of publications and information services for homeowners.

Continuing Care Accreditation Commission
901 E Street NW, Suite 500
Washington, DC 20004
202-783-7286
Lists of accredited housing by area. Confirms if facility is accredited. Brochure, *Ensuring Quality and Integrity in Continuing Care Retirement Communities.*

Federal Housing Administration
800-245-2691
Publications and names of local lenders participating in the FHA-insured reverse mortgage program.

National Center for Home Equity Conversion
7373 147th Street, West
Apple Valley, MN 55124
Reverse mortgages and other home equity conversion plans. Offers a reverse mortgage locator publication.

Shared Housing Resource Center
6344 Green Street
Philadelphia, PA 19144
215-848-1220
Information on shared housing. Assists in the development of group shared residences and shared housing matching services. Referrals to local organizations.

LEGAL MATTERS

American Bar Association
Commission on Legal Problems of the Elderly
740 15th Street NW, 8th Floor
Washington, DC 20005
202-662-8690
Booklets on Medigap insurance, advance medical directives, and housing rights of older people.

Equal Employment Opportunity Commission
800-669-4000
Information and assistance if you have been discriminated against by an employer.

Legal Assistance for Seniors
Contact your local Area Agency on Aging or the Elder Care Locator. Information on free legal services.

Legal Counsel for the Elderly
Sponsored by American Association of Retired People
601 E Street NW
Washington, DC 20049
202-434-2120
Publications such as *Organizing Your Future.*

Legal Services for the Elderly
132 West 43rd Street
New York, NY 10036
212-391-0120
An advisory center specializing in legal problems of older persons.
Publications.

National Academy of Elder Law Attorneys
1604 N. Country Club Road
Tucson, AZ 85716
520-881-4005 or 520-325-7925
National registry of attorneys who specialize in elder law. Pamphlet,
How to Choose an Elder Law Attorney.

National Senior Citizens Law Center
1815 K Street NW
Washington, DC 20006
202-887-5280
Information on legal problems of the elderly. Free consulting and
referrals.

Volunteer Lawyers Project
American Bar Association
740 15th Street NW, 8th Floor
Washington, DC 20005
202-662-8690
Answers to individuals' inquiries. Referrals to attorneys or others for assistance at little or no cost. Publications on legal problems of older people.

WORK AND RETIREMENT

American Craft Council
72 Spring Street
New York, NY 10012
212-274-0630
Information about events, courses, and local sources related to crafts.

American Hiking Society
1015 31st Street NW
Washington, DC 20007
703-385-3252
Lists of local hiking and trail clubs and brochure, *Hiking Safety.*

Association for Continuing Higher Education
c/o Executive Vice President
College of Graduate and Continuing Studies
Evansville University, Box 329
Evansville, IN 47702
812-479-2471
Information about adult education programs and courses; publications.

Elderhostel
75 Federal Street
Boston, MA 02110
617-426-7788
Catalog of educational trips for people over fifty in the United States and abroad.

Equal Employment Opportunity
800-669-4000
Local location and information to file a charge for age discrimination.

Institute of Lifetime Learning
AARP
1909 K Street
Washington, DC 20049
202-434-2277
Opportunities for older persons to continue to learn and prepare for new careers. Resource center. Publications such as *Learning Opportunities for Older Persons* and *College Centers for Older Learners*.

Interhostel
University of New Hampshire
6 Garrison Avenue
Durham, NH 03824
603-862-1147
An international travel-study program for adults fifty and over.

National Center on Arts and the Aging
409 3rd Street SW, Suite 200
Washington, DC 20024
202-479-1200
Information about the arts as activities available to older people.
Sponsors seminars and workshops.

National Displaced Homemakers Network
1625 K Street NW, Suite 300
Washington, DC 20006
202-467-6346
Information and assistance.

Senior Net
1 Kearny Street, 3rd Floor
San Francisco, CA 94108
415-352-1210
Nationwide network of people fifty-five and older using computers.
Newsletter, discounts on networking computer time, publications,
and a guide to using the network.

Service Corps of Retired Executives
409 3rd Street SW, 4th Floor
Washington, DC 20024
800-634-0245
Free business counseling. Referrals to local offices.

U.S. National Senior Olympics
14323 S. Outer Forty Road, Suite N300
Chesterfield, MO 63017
314-878-4900
Information on participating in the Senior Olympics.

BIBLIOGRAPHY

A Practical Guide to Choosing a Residential Care Home for the Elderly. Pamphlet published by Self-Help for the Elderly, San Francisco: 1992.

AARP's Catalog of Publications and Audiovisuals. American Association of Retired Persons. Washington, DC: 1995.

Aging Today. The bi-monthly newspaper of the American Society on Aging. San Francisco.

Atchley, Robert. *The Social Forces in Later Life: An Introduction to Social Gerontology.* Belmont: Wadsworth Publishing, 1980.

Barriers to Living Independently for Older Women with Disabilities. AARP, No. D14659, 1991.

Bateson, Mary Catherine. *Composing a Life.* New York: The Atlantic Monthly Press, 1990.

Before You Buy: A Guide To Long-Term Care Insurance. Health Advocacy Service Department, AARP, No. D12893, 1996.

Berg, Robert L. and Joseph S. Cassells, eds. *The Second Fifty Years: Promoting Health and Disability, The Institute of Medicine.* Washington DC: National Academy Press, 1990.

Berle, Gustav. *Retiring to Your Own Business: How You Can Launch a Satisfying, Productive and Prosperous Second Career.* Santa Maria: Puma Publishing, 1993.

Biracree, Tom and Nancy. *Over Fifty: The Resource Book for the Better Half of Your Life.* New York: Harper Perennial, 1991.

Bird, Caroline. *Lives of Our Own: Secrets of Salty Old Women.* Boston: Houghton Mifflin, 1995.

Birkedahl, Nonie. *Older and Wiser: A Workbook for Coping with Aging.* Oakland, CA: New Harbinger, 1991.

Braham, Barbara J. *Finding Your Purpose: A Guide to Personal Fulfillment.* Menlo Park: Crisp Publications, 1996.

Buckingham, Robert W. *The Complete Book of Home Health Care.* New York: Crossroads Publishing, 1984.

Bureau of Business Practice. *Complete Retirement Workshop: Your Guide to Planning a Secure and Rewarding Future.* Englewood Cliffs: Prentice Hall, 1993.

Burger, Sarah Greene and Martha D'erasmo. *Living in a Nursing Home: A Complete Guide for Residents, Their Families and Friends.* New York: Ballantine Books, 1976.

California Advocates for Nursing Home Reform. *A Consumer's Guide to Alternatives, Placement Considerations and Residents' Rights, Part 1.* San Francisco, 1993.

Callahan, Daniel. *Setting Limits: Medical Goals in an Aging Society.* Washington, DC: Georgetown University Press, 1987 and 1985.

Carter, Rosalynn with Susan K. Golant. *Helping Yourself Help Others.* New York: Times Books, 1994.

Chapman, Elwood N. *The Unfinished Business of Living.* Los Altos: Crisp Publications, 1988.

Clifford, Denis and Mary Randolf. *Who Will Handle Your Finances If You Can't?* Berkeley: Nolo Press, 1992.

Cohen, Donna, PhD, and Carl Eisdorfer, PhD, MD. *Seven Steps to Effective Parent Care.* New York: G.P. Putnam, 1993.

"Consider Nontraditional Households," *Womens' Initiative Newsletter,* AARP, No. D15549, Fall 1994.

Cooperman, Harriet. *Dying at Home.* New York: John Wiley & Sons, 1983, reprinted 1986.

Cort-Van Arsdale, Diana and Phyllis Newman. *Transitions: A Woman's Guide to Successful Retirement.* New York: Harper Collins, 1991.

Cross, Wilbur. *The Henry Holt Retirement Sourcebook: An Information Guide for Planning and Managing Your Affairs.* New York: Henry Holt, 1991.

Davis, Nancy D., Ellen Cole, and Esther D. Rothblum, eds. *Faces of Women and Aging.* New York: The Haworth Press, 1993.

DiMona, Lisa and Constance Herndon, eds. *The 1995 Information Please, Women's Sourcebook.* New York: Houghton Mifflin, 1995.

Doress-Worters, Paula B. and Diana Laskin Segal. *Ourselves, Growing Older.* New York: Simon & Schuster, 1994.

Downs, Hugh. *Fifty to Forever.* Nashville, TN: Thomas Nelson, 1994.

Erikson, Erik H., Joan M. Erikson, and Helen Q. Kivnick. *Vital Involvement in Old Age*. New York: Norton, 1986.

Fabry, Joseph B. *The Pursuit of Meaning: Viktor Frankl, Logotherapy, and Life*. New York: Harper & Row, 1980.

"Failing America's Caregivers: A Status Report on Women Who Care," Older Women's League, Washington, DC,1989.

Frankl, Viktor E. *Man's Search for Meaning: An Introduction to Logotherapy*. New York: Simon & Schuster, 1984.

Friedan, Betty. *The Fountain of Age*. New York: Simon and Schuster, 1993.

Friedman, Jo-Ann. *Home Health Care: A Complete Guide for Patients & Their Families*. New York: Fawcett Columbine, 1986.

Friends Can Be Good Medicine. California Department of Mental Health, 1981.

Frost, Robert. *The Road Not Taken*. New York: Holt, Rinehart and Winston, 1977.

Garner, J. Dianne, DSW, and Alice A. Young, PhD. "Women and Healthy Aging: Living Productively in Spite of It All." *Journal of Women and Aging* 5, nos. 3 and 4 (1993).

Guide to Choosing a Nursing Home. U.S. Department of Health and Human Services, Health Care Financing Administration, Publication No. HCFA-02174, 1994.

Guide to Health Insurance for People with Medicare. Developed jointly by the National Association of Insurance Commissioners and the Health Care Financing Administration, U.S. Department of Health and Human Services, Publication No. HCFA-02110, 1994.

Hasler, Bonnie Sether. *Barriers to Living Independently for Older Women with Disabilities.* AARP, No. D14659, 1991.

Hayes, Christopher L. and Jane M. Deren, eds. *Pre-retirement Planning for Women: Program Design and Research.* New York: Springer Publishing, 1990.

Haynes, Marion E., ed. *The Best of Retirement Planning.* Menlo Park: Crisp Publications, 1996.

Haynes, Marion E. *From Work to Retirement.* Menlo Park: Crisp Publications, 1996.

Health Promotion and Aging. U.S. Department of Health and Human Services, U.S. Government Printing Office, Publication ISBN 1-55672-006-8, 1986.

Helping Your Older Family Member Handle Finances. A Pacific Northwest Extension Publication, Oregon, Washington, Idaho, Publication PNW 344, 1989.

"Home Mortgages in Reverse: An Option for Elderly Homeowners," *Consumer Reports,* October 1992.

Homekeeper: It Pays to Keep You in Your Home. Fannie Mae Public Information Office, 3900 Wisconsin Avenue NW, Washington, DC 20016-2899, 1995.

Hooyman, Nancy R. and Wendy Lustbader. *Taking Care of Your Aging Family Members: A Practical Guide.* New York: The Free Press, 1986.

Hospice Benefits Under Medicare. Department of Health and Human Services, Publication No.: HFCA 02154, 1986.

"Housing and Living Arrangements," Womens' Initiative Fact Sheet, AARP, No. D15549, 1994.

Huttman, Elizabeth D. *Social Services for the Elderly.* New York: The Free Press, 1985.

If You Think You Need a Nursing Home: A Consumer's Guide to Financial Considerations and Medi-Cal Eligibility, Part 2. California Advocates for Nursing Home Reform, 1995.

"In-Home Supportive Services, Personal Care Services Program," Long-Term Care Fact Sheet, Public Interest Center on Long-Term Care, Sacramento, CA, 1994.

"Insurance to Pay for Long-Term Care," Susan Polniaszek, MPH, United Senior Health Cooperative, 1331 H Street NW, Suite 500, Washington, DC 20005.

Josefowitz, Natasha. *Is This Where I Was Going? Verses for Women in the Midst of Life.* New York: Warner Books, 1983.

Justice, Peggy O. *The Temp Track.* Princeton: Peterson's Pacesetters Books, 1993.

Kouri, Mary K., PhD. *Keys to Survival for Caregivers.* Hauppauge: Barron's Educational Series, 1992.

Leonard, Frances. *Money and the Mature Woman.* Reading, MA: Addison-Wesley, 1993.

Mace, Nancy L. and Peter V. Rabins, MD. *The 36-Hour Day.* Baltimore: Johns Hopkins University Press, 1981.

"Making Wise Decisions for Long-Term Care," AARP Health Advocacy Services Program Coordination and Development, No. D12435, 1992.

Manheimer, Ronald J., PhD. *The Second Middle Age: Looking Differently at Life Beyond Fifty.* Detroit: Visible Inc. Press, 1995.

"Marital Status and Living Arrangements," U.S. Bureau of the Census, Current Population Report Series P20-468, March 1992.

Martin, Charles L. *Your New Business: A Personal Plan for Success.* Menlo Park: Crisp Publications, 1996.

Martz, Sandra Haldeman, ed. *I Am Becoming the Woman I've Wanted.* Watsonville, CA: Papier-Mache Press, 1994.

"Medicare: An Overview," California Health Insurance Counseling and Advocacy Program, Los Angeles County, Publication 1/94A-001.

"Medicare, Q & A: 60 Commonly Asked Questions about Medicare," U.S. Department of Health and Human Services, Health Care Financing Administration, HCFA Publication No 02172, 1995.

Montgomery, Rhoda J.V. and Joyce Protero, eds. *Developing Respite Services for the Elderly*. Seattle: University of Washington Press, 1986.

Moody, H.R. *Aging*. Newbury Park: Sage Publications, 1996.

"Nursing Home Life: A Guide for Residents and Families," AARP, No. D13063, 1991.

Pastalan, Leon, PhD, ed. *Housing Decisions for the Elderly: To Move or Not to Move*. New York: The Haworth Press, 1995.

Pogrebin, Letty Cottin. *Getting Over Getting Older: An Intimate Journey*. Boston: Little, Brown, 1996.

Porcino, Jane. *Growing Older, Getting Better: A Handbook for Women in the Second Half of Life*. New York: Continuum, 1991.

"Practical Help for Those Caring for an Elderly Person in the Community: An Informal Caregiver's Curriculum," New York State Office for the Aging.

Rabin, David L. and Patricia Stockton. *Long-Term Care for the Elderly: A Factbook*. New York: Oxford University Press, 1987.

"Reverse Mortgage Locator," National Center for Home Equity Conversion, Apple Valley, MN, 1995.

Richards, Nanci B. and Betsy R. Schneier. *The Golden Horizons Retirement Guide*. Seattle, WA: Golden Horizons, 1988.

Robb, Caroline, RN, with Janet Reynolds, GNP. *The Caregiver's Guide: Helping Elderly Relatives Cope with Health & Safety Problems.* Boston: Houghton Mifflin, 1991.

Salman, John, PS, AIA. *The Do-able Renewable Home.* AARP, No. D12470, 1994.

Sarton, May. *At Seventy: A Journal.* New York: W.W. Norton, 1984.

Sheehy, Gail. *New Passages: Mapping Your Life Across Time.* New York: Random House, 1995.

Sinclair, Carole. *The Women's Retirement Book: Everything You Need to Know.* New York: Crown Trade Paperbacks, 1994.

"65+ in the United States," Bureau of the Census, Current Population Reports. April 1996.

Sommers, Tish and Laurie Shields. *Women Take Care: The Consequences of Caregiving in Today's Society.* Gainesville, TN: Triad Publishing, 1987.

"Staying at Home: A Guide to Long-Term Care and Housing," Program Coordination and Development Department, AARP, No. D14986, 1991.

Steinem, Gloria. *Moving Beyond Words.* New York: Simon & Schuster, 1994.

"Taking Care of Tomorrow: A Consumer's Guide to Long-Term Care," California Department of Aging, 1994.

Tatelbaum, Judy. *The Courage to Grieve.* New York: Harper & Row, 1980.

"Tomorrow's Choices: Preparing Now for Future Legal, Financial, and Health Care Decisions," AARP, No. D13479, 1991 (rev.).

U.S. Senate Special Committee on Aging, AARP, the Federal Council on the Aging, and the U.S. Administration on Aging. *Aging America: Trends and Projections.* 1991.

Vierck, Elizabeth. *Keys to Volunteering.* Hauppauge: Barrons Educational Services, 1996.

"Vital and Health Statistics." Center for Disease Control and Prevention/National Center for Health Statistics. Washington, DC: U.S. Government Printing Office, 1993.

Warner, Ralph. *Get a Life: You Don't Need a Million to Retire Well.* Berkeley: Nolo Press, 1996.

"Warning!! A Home Equity Loan May Be Hazardous to Your Home," Legal Assistance for Seniors, San Francisco, CA 1992.

"What Every Couple Should Know When One Spouse May Have to Enter a Nursing Home," Long-Term Care Fact Sheet, Public Interest Center on Long-Term Care, Sacramento, CA, 1994.

"When You Need a Nursing Home," *Age Page,* U.S. Department of Health and Human Services, U.S. Government Printing Office, Publication 491-280/4 0003, 1986.

"Your Medicare Handbook," Health Care Financing Administration, Office of Beneficiary Relations, N-1005, 7500 Security Boulevard, Baltimore, MD 21244-1850.

Zuckerman, Marilyn. *Poems of the Sixth Decade.* Cambridge, MA: Garden Strerity Bet Press, 1993.

INDEX

and safety adjustments, 69-70
Housing Act of 1974, 82
Housing and Urban Development
  Agency (HUD), 82
Huttman, Elizabeth
  Social Services for the Elderly, 150

Images, of women, 6, 11, 13
Immune system and psychosocial
  health, 33
Income
  annual, 49-52
  expanding, 56-57
Incontinence, urinary, 29
Institute of Medicine of the National
  Academy of Science, "The Second
  Fifty Years" (1990), 27
Insurance
  health, 53
  liability, 127, 129
  life, 54, 157
  long-term care, 53, 84, 86, 116,
    157-60
Interhostel, 106
Internal Revenue Service, 127
Internet, the
  as an educational tool, 105
Investment programs, 52-53
IRA (Individual retirement account), 51

Joint bank accounts, 117, 141

Keogh investment programs, 52

Learning and education opportunities,
  105-6
Legal Assistance for Seniors
  advice and help regarding:
    death of a care recipient, 140
    eligibility for Medicaid, 42
    nursing home contracts, 134
    power of attorney, 60, 117-18, 138,
      169
    reverse mortgages, 73

Legal issues
  in caregiving, 115-20
Leisure and recreation, 106-7
Leonard, Frances
  Money and the Mature Woman, 44
Liabilities, expenses, 49
Liability insurance, 127, 129
Life care communities, 85-86
Life expectancy, 3
Life insurance, 54
  and death notification, 141
  with "living benefits," 157
Lifestyle
  changes, 8, 14-16: in housing, 66-69;
    making a plan for, 37-38; in
    retirement, 87-107
  choices, 14-15, 16
  and health maintenance, 21
  and health problems, 29-35
Living trust, 59, 118-19
Living will, 138, 169-70
Logotherapy, 89
Long-term care, 39
  in advancing years, 156-62
  insurance for, 53, 84, 86, 157-60
  physical and emotional demands of
    caregivers in, 101-101, 114-15,
    135-41
  veterans' benefits for, 116, 133-34

Malnutrition, 31
Meals on Wheels, 31, 125, 126, 127,
  154
Medicaid, 39, 40, 41, 129, 133
  and assisted living, 84
  and the Department of Welfare, 126
  and long-term care, 156-57, 160-61
  and nursing home care, 86, 116-17, 119
  nursing home certification, 132-34
  and the QMB program, 160-61
  Supplemental Security Income, 51,
    151, 160
Medical. *See also* Health
  assessment, 36-37

ABOUT THE AUTHORS

LUCY SCOTT, PHD, a psychologist, educator, and author, has devoted thirty-five years to educating women of all ages. Having earned a PhD in psychology from the Fielding Institute in Santa Barbara, she was a faculty member of the California School of Professional Psychology and has had a private therapy and consultation practice specializing in women's issues and life planning. She coauthored *Time Out for Motherhood: A Guide to the Financial, Emotional, and Career Aspects of Having a Baby* with Meredith Angwin (Jeremy P. Tarcher, 1986). A member of the Older Women's League, the American Psychological Association, the American Society on Aging, and Who's Who in American Women, she has appeared on national television and radio and been quoted often in newspaper and magazine articles as a leading expert on women's lives. Lucy lives in Berkeley, California, with her husband and is the mother of two daughters and three stepchildren, and the grandmother of nine.

KERSTIN JOSLYN SCHREMP, PHD, is a retired sociologist, educator, and retirement planning consultant. She earned a PhD in sociology and education from the University of California at Berkeley and was a full professor and chair of the Sociology Department at Dominican College in San Rafael, California, for many years. She headed the NOW National Task Force on Women and Volunteerism in 1972 and cowrote the position paper. Kerstin is married and the mother of three children and one stepchild, and the grandmother of four.

BETTY SOLDZ, BSW, a social worker and health educator, is an Older Adult Services consultant and a volunteer counselor and community educator with the Health Insurance Counseling and Advocacy Program of California. She facilitates workshops and support groups for seniors and actively advocates for older women as chairperson and board member of a local chapter of the Older Women's League. She is also a member of the Gray Panthers, the American Society on Aging, the National Council of Senior Citizens, and California Advocates for Nursing Home Reform. Betty lives with her husband of forty-nine years in Berkeley, California. She is the mother of two sons and has one grandson.

BARBARA WEISS, MSW, has forty-five years experience as a social worker, educator, administrator, and community leader. She has been a faculty member of the School of Social Welfare at the University of California at Berkeley for the past twenty-eight years, both as a teacher and as a consultant developing internships for social welfare graduate students. She has also led workshops for national conferences for the Older Women's League and for the American Society on Aging, and she served as regional vice president of the National Association of Social Workers. A founding board member of CHOICE: Institute for Women in Mid-Life Transition, she is also a board member of the Women's Foundation, serving low-income and minority women in northern California. Barbara is a wife, mother, grandmother, and great-grandmother.

MORE PAPIER-MACHE PRESS TITLES OF RELATED INTEREST

Old Is Not a Four-Letter Word: A Midlife Guide

Ann E. Gerike, PhD

Illustrations by Peter Kohlsaat

Thirty-five million baby boomers are fast approaching the Big Five-Oh. This humorous, down-to-earth text demolishes negative myths about aging, instead describing enriching changes and opportunities. Liberally accompanied by Peter Kohlsaat's cartoons, this book is powerful enough to change attitudes about aging for a lifetime.

"Ann Gerike has some serious messages for us about the myths and realities of aging but delivers them with abundant wit and humor. Laugh and learn with Old Is Not a Four-Letter Word.*"* —Robert N. Butler, MD, Professor and Director, International Longevity Center (U.S.), Dept. of Geriatrics and Adult Development, The Mount Sinai Medical Center

ISBN 1-57601-002-3, trade paper

A Time to Say Good-Bye: Moving Beyond Loss

Mary Goulding, MSW

Mary Goulding, an internationally recognized psychotherapist, recounts her own very human journey through the process of mourning the death of her husband—her partner both professionally and privately. This book is for anyone who has experienced loss, and must relearn how to enjoy a rich, full life.

"One of the best books I've read on grieving. One of the best I've read on living." —Jeffrey K. Zeig, PhD, Director, The Milton H. Erickson Foundation

ISBN 0-918949-74-2, trade paper

Grow Old Along with Me—The Best Is Yet to Be
Edited by Sandra Haldeman Martz
In the enriching tradition of her million-copy bestseller, *When I Am an Old Woman I Shall Wear Purple*, Sandra Martz rewards us with her latest celebration of aging. This eloquent collection appreciates the similarities and differences between men and women aging, transforming our myths of aging into a real sense of wonder and expectation.
"Nothing could be more timely than this book." —Studs Terkel, author of *Coming of Age*
"Read, feel the life in this book, and let it help you create a life of poetry and story." —Bernie Siegel, MD, author of *Love, Medicine, and Miracles*
ISBN 0-918949-86-6, trade paper
ISBN 0-918949-87-4, hardcover

Learning to Sit in the Silence: A Journal of Caretaking
Elaine Marcus Starkman
Writer and teacher Elaine Marcus Starkman addresses the issue of caring for aging relatives in this moving book. Based on her experiences caring for her aging mother-in-law over a ten-year period, *Learning to Sit in the Silence* reveals in journal form the day-to-day joys and challenges of caregiving.
"...for everyone who loves life and recognizes that caregiving takes strength, fortitude, compassion, and a whole lot of love." —Phyllis J. Lessin, Asst. Chief, Alzheimer's Disease Research Center, UC San Diego
ISBN 0-918949-43-2, trade paper
ISBN 0-918949-44-0, hardcover

Time for Love: Assisted Living Viewed by One of the Very Old
Janet Carncross Chandler
As a noted poet and retired social worker, Chandler provides a rare expert insider's perspective of living in a long-term care facility. Describing her transition from living independently to living with assistance, her poetic reflections resonate with elegance and insight.
"Janet Chandler's poems and prose give hope—hope that we too can balance the physical decline and loss of later life with a flourish of creativity and productivity." —Joanne Smallen, MSW, gerontologist
ISBN 0-918949-91-2, trade paper

Kitchen Tables (and Other Midlife Musings)
Niela Eliason
Niela Eliason captures the lively essence of daily life and its accompanying memories for anyone in their midlife years. These essays are a treasure chest of the insightful thoughts, feelings, and opinions of our middle-aged generation—trusting chicken soup, staying married, and sharing stories around the kitchen table.
"Have a seat at Niela Eliason's kitchen table. You'll enjoy the stories she's going to tell you." —Tony Hillerman
ISBN 0-918949-62-9, trade paper

PAPIER-MACHE PRESS

At Papier-Mache Press, it is our goal to identify and successfully present important social issues through enduring works of beauty, grace, and strength. Through our work we hope to encourage empathy and respect among diverse communities, creating a bridge of understanding between the mainstream audience and those who might not otherwise be heard.

We appreciate you, our customer, and strive to earn your continued support. We also value the role of the bookseller in achieving our goals. We are especially grateful to the many independent booksellers whose presence ensures a continuing diversity of opinion, information, and literature in our communities. We encourage you to support these bookstores with your patronage.

We publish many fine books about women's experiences. We also produce lovely posters and T-shirts that complement our anthologies. Please ask your local bookstore which Papier-Mache items they carry. To receive our complete catalog, send your request to Papier-Mache Press, 627 Walker Street, Watsonville, CA 95076, or call our toll-free number, 800-927-5913.